"I have been married for forty-eight years. But even now, a half-century later, the days of falling in love and 'going with' Noël are still vivid in my memory. They are in a class by themselves. Marriage knows its unfettered ecstasies, but those years leading to marriage were supercharged with never-before and never-since emotions. We need God's wisdom. And we need his supernatural help to live it out. Marshall Segal is a trustworthy guide. He is conscious of the world but conformed to the Word. God did not leave us without wisdom or power for this volatile season of life. Marshall will point you to both."

John Piper, founder, desiringGod.org; Chancellor, Bethlehem College & Seminary

"Singleness is not a punishment, and marriage is not a right. Yet more and more, I encounter young women who are single longer than they planned to be, and they wonder how they missed the dreamboat. What's more, they wonder why God hasn't answered their prayers for marriage. That's why I'm thrilled to get my hands on *Not Yet Married*. This is a book not just about waiting well or about preparing for marriage. It is a book about God, grounded in God's Word. Married, engaged, or a long way away from the altar, this book paints a beautiful, biblical picture of marriage and the God who designed it."

Erin L. Davis, blogger; Bible teacher; author, *Beyond Bath Time*; *True Princess*; and *Beautiful Encounters*

"This is a book about God and his glory before it is a field guide for the not yet married. That will be its sticking power. Segal has done a great job of connecting gospel truth to how we think about ourselves and our love lives, which is desperately needed in a culture that wants to keep God sequestered to the sanctuary. It's weighty but accessible, taking on serious topics in a way that reads like a chat over coffee. I know the title is *Not Yet Married*, but after eleven years of marriage I found myself challenged and encouraged on every page. I am really grateful for Marshall and his honest, theologically sturdy counsel. This book is a must-share."

Jimmy Needham, recording artist; Worship Director, Stonegate Church, Midlothian, Texas

"Marshall's writing never fails to be richly insightful, thought provoking, and heart probing. He is also refreshingly transparent as he shares out of what he has experienced—sometimes the hard way—of God's Word and ways. As Marshall chronicled his journey through years of singleness, I was delighted to see God bring Faye into his life 'in due season.' Now I rejoice that he has written this book, which will be a feast to men and women in any season of life, as they press through every unfulfilled longing this side of heaven, to pursue joy in Christ."

Nancy DeMoss Wolgemuth, host, *Revive Our Hearts*; author, *Lies Women Believe and the Truth That Sets Them Free*; *A Place of Quiet Rest*; and *Seeking Him*

"Timely. Relevant. Solid. In a cultural climate where singleness is equally celebrated and stigmatized, and dating is misunderstood and mispurposed, Marshall Segal injects a breath of biblical fresh air. With Scripture as its undergirding, *Not Yet Married* is a helpful guide to honoring God in any relational status. Married or not, single or dating, I hope you'll read this book."

Louie Giglio, Pastor, Passion City Church, Atlanta; founder, Passion Conferences; author, *The Comeback*

"In a culture that constantly communicates false—even destructive—messages about dating, *Not Yet Married* is the Christian response we need. Marshall is deeply biblical and writes with the empathy, humility, and wisdom of a brother who has walked this road, made mistakes, and found grace. Now he shares his experience and gospel-rich insights with us. Teenagers especially will benefit from Marshall's words. For that reason, this book will be one I joyfully recommend far and wide."

Jaquelle Crowe, Lead Writer and Editor in Chief, TheRebelution.com; contributor, The Gospel Coalition; author, *This Changes Everything*

"For years, I've longed for a book I could recommend without hesitation to single men and women. My wait is over. Marshall Segal's *Not Yet Married* is everything I hoped for and more. His foundations are thoroughly scriptural, his applications are rooted in the good news of the gospel, and he provides some of the clearest counsel for navigating the unmarried years I've ever seen. He humbly acknowledges his own failures and addresses past sins with sensitive pastoral skill. If you're single, this book will increase your faith in God's good plans for you and inspire you to passionately pursue a Christ-exalting life. I can't wait to recommend and give this book away."

Bob Kauflin, Director of Worship, Sovereign Grace Ministries; elder, Sovereign Grace Church, Louisville; author, *Worship Matters* and *True Worshipers*

"Instead of settling for our culture's cheap version of love, sex, and dating, *Not Yet Married* challenges and inspires Christian singles to live their lives with greater intentionality. This down-to-earth book is a must-read for every guy and girl who desires to glorify God to the fullest while they're not yet married."

Kristen Clark and Bethany Baird, founders, GirlDefined Ministries; authors, *Girl Defined*

Not Yet Married

NOT YET MARRIED

The Pursuit of Joy in Singleness and Dating

MARSHALL SEGAL

:: CROSSWAY®

WHEATON, ILLINOIS

Not Yet Married: The Pursuit of Joy in Singleness and Dating

Copyright © 2017 by Marshall Segal

Published by Crossway
        1300 Crescent Street
        Wheaton, Illinois 60187

Cover design: Tim Green, Faceout Studio

Cover image: Roy Margaliot / offset.com

First printing 2017

Printed in the United States of America

Scripture quotations are from the ESV® Bible (The Holy Bible, English Standard Version®), copyright © 2001 by Crossway, a publishing ministry of Good News Publishers. Used by permission. All rights reserved.

All emphases in Scripture quotations have been added by the author.

Trade paperback ISBN: 978-1-4335-5545-9
ePub ISBN: 978-1-4335-5548-0
PDF ISBN: 978-1-4335-5546-6
Mobipocket ISBN: 978-1-4335-5547-3

Library of Congress Cataloging-in-Publication Data

Names: Segal, Marshall, 1986– author.
Title: Not yet married : the pursuit of joy in singleness and dating / Marshall Segal.
Description: Wheaton : Crossway, 2017. | Includes bibliographical references and index.
Identifiers: LCCN 2016032848 (print) | LCCN 2017013275 (ebook) | ISBN 9781433555466 (pdf) | ISBN 9781433555473 (mobi) | ISBN 9781433555480 (epub) | ISBN 9781433555459 (tp)
Subjects: LCSH: Single people—Religious life. | Dating (Social customs)—Religious aspects—Christianity.
Classification: LCC BV4596.S5 (ebook) | LCC BV4596.S5 S44 2017 (print) | DDC 248.8/4—dc23
LC record available at https://lccn.loc.gov/2016032848

Crossway is a publishing ministry of Good News Publishers.

VP		28	27	26	25	24	23	22	21	20	19	18
17	16	15	14	13	12	11	10	9	8	7	6	5

To Ellis Kai
Married or not,
may your heart be God's

Contents

Introduction

We live and date in a society of now. We can watch anything we want, anytime we want, anywhere we want. We can have any kind of food delivered to our front door in minutes. And we can "like," flirt, and text from the safety and comfort of the crumb-filled couch in our bachelor pad. The same selfishness and impatience are also the main ingredients in a tidal wave of premarital sex, leading more than half of us to give ourselves away before we even graduate high school. With a little computer-generated imagery, it all looks like unfenced and unfiltered freedom and adventure. But what if we're missing a fuller freedom and a greater adventure while we settle for something quicker, easier, and cheaper? What if we realized we were skipping all-you-can-eat meat at a Brazilian steakhouse for a few stray Froot Loops at the breakfast table?

As we look at dating, even in the church, we have to admit that too many of us have got it all wrong. We hurry to date as soon as we hit high school but wait to settle down and marry until after we've started our career and enjoyed some freedom. We come in and out of relationships like buying new shoes, slipping off anyone who begins to feel uncomfortable or inconvenient and then picking up whatever pair we like best the next day. Most of the time we like the idea of saving ourselves sexually, but not in the most important moments. Meanwhile, the world is always inventing new and easier-to-use technology to help us give ourselves away too soon to someone we don't even know. We love to be loved but aren't completely sure we even know what love is.

The whole dating game thrives on adrenaline and ambiguity—always showing enough to pique someone's interest and curiosity, but never enough to answer the most important questions. It's a game of cat-and-mouse without any mice (and I think we can all agree there's nothing worse than a room full of cats). We bait each other with half-truths about the best parts of ourselves, always selecting exactly what to show and how to show it, only revealing what might entice or intrigue each other. Dating today also tends to center the whole world around me—my interests, my friends, my preferences. Many of us think we're pursuing marriage as we chat and flirt with one another, but we're really just pursuing ourselves—our own image and self-esteem, our own selfish desires, and our own ego. We're always projecting and positioning ourselves to get the attention and affirmation we crave but without ever risking or giving up too much in the process.

Jesus invites us to love and date differently, in ways that resist and rise above almost every trend among the not yet married today. When worth and identity are being measured in society by who likes us and how many like us, he reminds us we're already worth far more than we know and defined by a love higher than any human love. Against all the hide-and-seek ambiguity, he injects us with intentionality—with the liberty to communicate clearly and carefully in love and the luxury to know and be known in relationships. While so many recklessly mingle in this me-generation, he sets us free from selfishness, showing us how to put others' interests, needs, and hearts before our own, and teaching us to refuse to satisfy ourselves at others' expense. And when everyone else feels entitled to have everything now, he sets us apart as the strange and strong who are willing and eager to wait. If Christian dating—the intentional, selfless, and prayerful process of pursuing marriage—sounds like slavery, we don't get it. If low-commitment sexual promiscuity sounds like freedom, we don't get it. Jesus may ask more of us, but he does so to secure something far better for us.

Not Yet Married

Some of you will readily identify with the title of this book, and others will be offended by the label. If you're in the latter group, you are probably reading through this introduction not so secretly wanting to validate your utter dissatisfaction with such a shallow view of singleness. Why would we define ourselves by the absence of marriage, especially when many of us are children of the living God through faith in Jesus, bought at infinite price, filled with divine power, and promised an eternity of life and happiness?

Even though I responded that way to married advice and encouragement at times during my single years—"Stop defining me by my singleness!"—I've come to like the phrase "not yet married" for at least four reasons. First, there are lots of Christians who do have a deep and enduring desire for marriage, people whose hearts ache to find a husband or a wife. It's a calling they believe God has put on their life, yet it remains an unrealized and unconfirmed calling today. Many of them have tried to pursue marriage the right way—not diving in too quickly, setting clear standards and boundaries, and leaning in to good friends and counselors. But it hasn't worked out. The dates they have been on haven't gone well, or no one's ever shown any interest. Others have thrown themselves into relationship after relationship, dragged around by their desires for intimacy and led into any manner of sexual immorality and regret. They've been told their desire is good, but they have no idea how to take the next step, or how to think about all these months or years of brokenness and loneliness. That may not be you, but it was me, and it's probably at least a few of your Christian friends. I want to shape our waiting and longing to reflect everything Jesus has *already* given and promised us, and to honor the work he's given us to do in every season of life, regardless of our marital status.

Second, statistically most of you will be married. A few of you will be called to lifelong singleness, and it will be a beautiful thing to watch you savor Christ and serve others as a single man or woman. It will be a stunning thing for the world to see, someone trading the pleasure of marital love and sexual intimacy for a lifetime of loving God and laying down his or her life to bring others to Christ. But most of you will be married, even if that's not on your radar or priority list today. If trends from the last couple hundred years continue, the average believer will be married at some point in life. Therefore, it seems appropriate to talk to most believers in their twenties or thirties as if they might one day be married. We should not be consumed by that reality, define our progress or contentment by our marital status, or give all of ourselves to pursuing marriage. We should, however, prepare ourselves to be ready and faithful if God calls us to love and serve a husband or wife.

Some of you are not convinced. You're still skeptical and offended. Ironically, that's another reason I've come to like the phrase "not yet married." More and more, young people are disillusioned with and pessimistic about marriage. There are several factors here, I am sure. Divorce may be the biggest. Many of us have tasted divorce firsthand as children, or watched our friends suffer from it. Why would I think *my* marriage would survive? Why would I subject myself to that kind of regret and pain? I want at least a few of you to believe again in marriage. One of the most radical and countercultural things we can do today to declare our faith in Jesus is to marry someone and remain faithful to that spouse until we die.

Finally, on this side of heaven we are all not yet married. Every wedding day is only a small and inadequate picture of a wedding day to come, when we are given again forever to our Savior and

King. On *that* day, we will sing, "Let us rejoice and exult and give him the glory, for the marriage of the Lamb has come, and his Bride has made herself ready" (Rev. 19:7). God made our marriages to be movie posters of a marriage to come. The way we love a husband or wife, as imperfectly as we will love him or her, says a *lot* about the kind of love God has for us, but it will be nothing compared to the real thing—an eternity of peace, joy, and life purchased for us by our Bridegroom at the cross. One day we'll get to meet him face-to-face. It will be the greatest family reunion of all time—the wedding to end all weddings—when God with open arms receives broken us, made beautiful by the blood of Jesus. We *will* all be married, and that marriage should shape every other desire and longing we have in this life.

Not Yet Married is *not* about dwelling on the negative. If we are in Christ, we are never again defined by what we are not. We have too much in him to be discouraged about not having anything else—even things as important in this life as a job or a spouse or children. The things that fill our lives and make us happy here are simple grains of sand compared to the endless beaches of knowing Christ. It *was*, after all, an unmarried man who said, "I count everything as loss because of the surpassing worth of knowing Christ Jesus my Lord. For his sake I have suffered the loss of all things and count them as rubbish, in order that I may gain Christ and be found in him" (Phil. 3:8–9).

My Not-Yet-Married Story

I wanted to be married long before I could even drive. Maybe I watched too many Disney movies. Maybe the "burn" just began too early for me (1 Cor. 7:9). I believe the desire was born, at least in my best moments, watching my parents love each other. My parents are not perfect, and their marriage has not been perfect, but the lasting pictures in my head from my childhood are of them happy together—kissing when Dad got home from work, reading together in the living room night after night, loving their sons, laughing at each other's lame jokes, sitting down most mornings to read the Bible and pray together, even if for just a few minutes. I saw the friendship and romance they enjoyed, and I dreamed of finding that for myself.

It was a good desire, but it did not produce many good things in immature me. In fact, nothing in my life and faith has been more confusing and spiritually hazardous than my pursuit of marriage. From far too young, I longed for the affection, safety, and intimacy I anticipated with a wife. Sadly, those desires predictably did much more harm than good. I started dating too early. I stayed in relationships too long. I experimented too much with our hearts and allowed things to go too far. I said "I love you" too soon. I desperately searched for love but without my heart and hope anchored in Christ. So I would always end up back where I started, alone, only more insecure and ashamed. I sinned against and hurt a number of young women along the way because I was led along and blinded by my own selfishness instead of leading well in relationships like a caring and self-controlled son of God. So, when God withheld marriage from me long into my twenties, my singleness became a regular reminder, for more than a decade, that I had messed up, missed opportunities, and done it wrong.

I met Alyssa Faye Nera on October 11, 2012, a day before we walked side by side in someone else's wedding, just a groomsman and a bridesmaid. We were married two and a half years later. I was twenty-nine. She was twenty-eight. I wrote a lot of this book, and learned almost all of the lessons, before I married my wife. God taught me a lot through her over those two years, especially through her contentment in and with Jesus, her prayerfulness, and her zeal for purity. My relationship with Faye was an unexpected, undeserved anomaly in my broken search for marriage. A good deal of our story will be scattered throughout the book, but our dating, engagement, and now marriage is a story of God healing what was broken, restoring what had been lost, redeeming what had gone wrong, and building something entirely new.

Looking back, I'm convinced God did withhold marriage to discipline me—not to *punish* me but to prepare me and mature me as a man and as a future husband. I also believe he withheld marriage to draw me closer to himself and to allow me to use my gifts to serve others while I was still single. Because of that, *Not Yet Married* is not a book about waiting quietly in the corner of the world for God to bring a spouse, but it is about mobilizing you—a growing generation and movement of single men and women—out of shame, selfishness, and self-pity into deeper levels of love for Christ and more consistent and creative ministry to others.

The Not-Yet-Married Life

This is a book for not-yet-married people that's not mainly about marriage, or even dating. I set out to write a book *for* not-yet-married men and women *about God*, and about our role in his world. Instead of being *mainly* about do's and don'ts and not yets, the book is meant to inspire and deploy single you with what God has for you now. The first half of the book focuses on the not-yet-married life—on a sense of joy, purpose, and belonging in singleness. I desperately want you to know that you were made for more than marriage—that marriage will never satisfy or fulfill your deepest needs and cravings. That hole in our hearts will swallow and destroy any relationship if we look to a person to make us happy or whole. And I say that as someone who chased marriage for years, relationship after relationship, searching for love, worth, and identity in a wife. These chapters address singleness in the not-yet-married life, but they will not speak to every single person's situation. Singleness takes on different forms and different trials over time. My not-yet-married story started in my teens and lasted through my twenties, so I am writing mainly with young people in mind. If that's not you, you might be disappointed that I don't talk to you more, but I hope you also resonate with and take away more than you expected.

I could have written another book just about dating, but I didn't. I wrote about *singleness* and dating, because the most important things I learned in singleness and dating were not about dating or marriage. They were about life and God, about finding *real* purpose and *real* satisfaction deeper than any romance. Marriage does not unlock God's plans and purposes for us. He sends us into the world when he saves us, not when he watches us walk down the aisle. Not-yet-married Christians are not junior varsity Christians. You're as Christian as any other Christian—the same Savior rescuing us from wasting our lives, the same Spirit making us new and equipping us to make a difference, the same mission to tell the whole world about Jesus.

In the second half of the book, we'll focus on dating. We'll start by rebuilding a vision of marriage that eclipses the small, shallow pictures we see in movies and on television. We'll ask what makes marriage something worth wanting. The reality is, many of us want it for wrong or second-rate reasons. Others are ready to pass altogether. But God did something uniquely and stunningly beautiful when he brought man and woman *together*. And we will never date well until we have a big, clear, and compelling idea of what marriage was really meant to be. The rest of the chapters slowly turn the diamond of Christian dating, looking at what makes this kind of dating dramatically different. How do I know he's the one? Where should we set boundaries in our relationship? What do I do when she breaks up with me? We want to date in a way that makes Jesus look real and reliable to others around us.

We're in the pursuit of joy, not marriage. Before anyone could ever make us happy in marriage, we have to have already given our hearts away. The surest love, the fullest happiness, and the highest purpose are all available to you in Jesus, just as you are.

Find them first in him, and you will have a far happier and more meaningful marriage, if God brings you a husband or wife one day. And if, in his wisdom and his unfailing love for you, he chooses not to, not-yet-married you will enjoy more than you ever could have dreamed or found for yourself apart from him.

Part I

THE NOT-YET-MARRIED LIFE

1

Love Is Looking for You

We are all wired to want happiness, love, and significance. We all want our hearts to soar for something. We taste happiness in lots of things—in the first bite of a slightly undercooked brownie, in an overtime playoff win, in a new dress or pair of shoes—but the joy is always just enough to know we're made for something more. Every joy here carries some kind of empty, unsatisfying aftertaste. Wrapped up with that desire to be happy is a desire to be known and loved. Our life was formed and given to us to be shared. We are all designed for relationship, regardless of whether we're married. And we all want our lives to count for something. We want to contribute something significant to a meaningful cause. We want to make a difference. Discontentment and disappointment rise up in the not-yet-married life when we start pursuing that love, joy, and significance in a person and not in God. We become miserable *not* because we're not married, but because many of us think marriage might finally make us happy.

If you had asked me when I was twenty what would make me happy, I was already Christian enough to say, "Jesus." I knew the right answer. But if anyone watched my life closely enough back then and could answer for me, they probably would have said, "Marriage." I went to church every Sunday. I had quiet times. I was doing ministry to high school guys. I really did love Jesus. But, if I'm honest, I gave more of myself to girls than to God. I really wanted to be married, and I loved the attention, affection, and security of having a girlfriend. I had already plunged myself into one long serious relationship after another for five or six years—five or six first dates, five or six premature first kisses, five or six devastating breakups. I didn't experiment with marijuana or go through a drinking phase. My drug of choice was more socially acceptable, even encouraged. I was recklessly trying to feed my heart's hunger for God by running after romance and intimacy.

I began each new relationship under the banner of "my pursuit of marriage," but much of it was really just my pursuit of me. I loved the idea of marriage, because I thought marriage would fill and complete *me*. But because I was looking for love, happiness, and significance mainly in marriage, singleness turned into a nightmare some days. Singleness felt lonely, waiting for someone to come into my life and never leave again. Singleness felt incomplete, wondering if God would bring my other half or fill the massive, glaring hole in my life (at least it looked massive and glaring in the mirror). Singleness provoked self-pity, wanting what others already had, and thinking I deserved it more than them. Relationships towered above all my idols, so singleness became simultaneously my unrelenting judge and unwanted roommate, reminding me at all times of what I didn't have yet and what I didn't do right.

The American-Dream Marriage

The Bible says that people who are fixated on experiencing as much happiness and pleasure as possible here on earth—in a career, in sex, drinking, or spending, even in marriage—are like those who dream they are eating and drinking, but wake up hungry, thirsty, and without anything to eat or drink (Isa. 29:8). The beautiful banquet before their unconscious and closed eyelids—perfectly grilled meats, colorful and fresh fruits and vegetables, bread right out of the oven, the fountain of wine, chocolate filled with chocolate, drizzled with chocolate—is all just a mirage, a cruel figment of a hungry person's imagination. For the not yet married, the imaginary buffet might feature a good-looking, funny, considerate, and committed spouse, two or maybe three children, the house you always wanted, summer vacations somewhere nice, and blissful married memory after blissful married memory—the American-dream marriage. But every delicious dream must end.

The problem is not that we are hungry but that we're hunting in the wrong pantry. The cravings deep inside us are a *mercy* from God meant to lead us to God. God is trying to give us unconditional love, indescribable joy, and unparalleled purpose, but many of us are just trying to get married. "Blessed are those who hunger and thirst for righteousness, for they shall be satisfied" (Matt. 5:6). God wired appetites—intense biological, emotional, sexual, spiritual, unavoidable desires—into every human soul so that *he* could fill them. He wants us to be full, not empty; to be loved, not lonely. One of my favorite verses in the Bible says, "In your presence there is fullness of joy; at your right hand are pleasures forevermore" (Ps. 16:11). No greater joy. No expiration date. Happiness and love like this are free—"by grace you have been saved" (Eph. 2:5, 8)—but it is not cheap. It takes patience, hard work, and perseverance—day after day, pouring ourselves into God's Word, sacrificing for the sake of others in his name, and surrendering ourselves to his will. Paul calls the Christian life a fight and a race (2 Tim. 4:7). It can be hard, and it may hurt along the way, but we'll never regret it. Jesus may ask a lot of us between here and heaven, but whether we ever get married or not, he will give it all back a hundredfold and more (Matt. 19:29).

Believe in Love, Again

At least part of what makes singleness so lonely and miserable is that we have such a hard time believing someone like God could really, genuinely love someone like us. Some of us have experienced so little love in this life that we don't have categories for what that would even feel like. We've been abandoned by parents, betrayed by friends, or left behind by another boyfriend or girlfriend. Marriage feels like one last-ditch effort to find love, but deep inside we're terrified we'll just find more of the same. We simply cannot imagine being truly, deeply, and consistently loved. And then God says, "I love you." Really?

God does love you. "See what kind of love the Father has given to us, that we should be called children of God; and so we are" (1 John 3:1). We are prized sons and daughters. God loved us even though we never deserved his love (Rom. 5:8). You and I were dead without Christ—not wrong, not sick, not stupid, but dead. "You were *dead* in the trespasses and sins in which you once walked" (Eph. 2:1–2). We were absolutely, stubbornly unlovable. "*But God*, being rich in mercy, because of the great love with which he loved us, even when we were dead in our trespasses, made us alive together with Christ—by grace you have been saved" (vv. 4–5). God found you dead in your sin, in full rebellion against him, utterly hopeless, and he loved you to life and made you his own. He was willing to send his Son to a cross for you to show you what real love looks like and to give you a reason to believe in love, again.

This love will never leave you or forsake you (Heb. 13:5). He will never call to break up with you. He will never walk out on you like your dad walked out on your family. He never lies, and he will never die, leaving you behind and alone. In fact, *nothing* can take this love away from you (Rom. 8:38–39). If you are hidden in Christ through faith, God loves you, and nothing and no one can stop him from loving you. God has plans for you, good plans better than anything you could dream or want for yourself. "No eye has seen, nor ear heard, nor the heart of man imagined, what God has prepared for those who love him" (1 Cor. 2:9). Your Father loves you, far more than a future spouse ever will or could.

God Made You on Purpose

The God who loves you also made you. He designed you—your physique, your personality, every inch of you—and knows you completely (Ps. 139:14–15). You were not an accident. You were created in love and on purpose. *But why did God make me, and what did he want me to do?* A lot of us start asking that question more seriously in college. I remember I had to dream a little harder my sophomore year when Wake Forest University made me declare a major. It felt like I was deciding what to do with the rest of my life—fifty or more *years* on the line. I sat and stared at three candidates: education, business, and Christian studies. At the time, it seemed like education would make me happy, business would make Dad happy, and Christian studies would make God happy. Ultimately, I chose business. But that same sophomore year, in the midst of all the accounting, human resources, and marketing, God was teaching me why I was made and how he wanted me to spend the rest of my life, regardless of whether I was a teacher, an account executive, or a pastor—and regardless of whether I ever got married.

Every single person on the planet was made to say something about God. The Creator and Sustainer of the universe made each of us, and filled us, along with the other seven billion people on the planet, with a purpose. Most of us have a hard time really believing we were created *by someone*, and for something far bigger than ourselves. We're raised, trained, and spent in a much smaller world, a world centered on ourselves and reaching only as far as we can see. But God made you and me for far more than marriage, business, or whatever else we each might choose for ourselves. If we miss this, we risk wasting our lives running in wrong directions, pursuing pitiful dreams, and serving tiny gods. The earlier we answer the biggest questions about our life, though, the better we'll answer all the smaller ones—like what we will study, where we will work, and whom we will marry.

A lot of us want to keep God close enough to save us but far enough away to let us do what we want to do. But we have to be brave enough to ask why God made us in the first place. With this question, it really does help to start in the beginning. "In the beginning, God . . ." (Gen. 1:1). The Bible doesn't begin with Adam. It begins with God. God is the author, the painter, the creator in this story—in every person's story. So, why did God create you? "Then God said, 'Let us make man *in our image*, after our likeness.' . . . So God created man *in his own image, in the image of God* he created him; male and female he created them" (Gen. 1:26–27). Why did God make you? He repeats himself three times to make himself clear. He made you in his image, in his likeness—*to look like him*. Why does someone make anything in someone else's image—a painting, a sculpture, an Instagram?[1] Why do we create things that image or look like others—our parents, our best friends, our favorite athletes or artists? Because we want to see them, and we want others to see them. Why did God make you? That question is infinitely more important than asking whom we will marry (or even *if* we will marry). The shortest answer is that we were meant to show others a bit of who God is, to share and display the love we've experienced with him. We're seven billion Instagrams of God.

A Love Too Good Not to Share

Made in the image of God, we're meant to be living, breathing pictures of him and his glory—his beauty, his integrity, his mercy, his justice, his love (Isa. 43:7). We were formed and made on purpose, for a purpose. The most important thing we could accomplish here on earth, then, is to give ourselves completely to telling the world with our whole life that God is truer, greater, and more satisfying than our wildest imagination—than the most successful career, the biggest platform, or the happiest marriage.

So how do we live for God and his glory? We don't *make* God glorious or add any glory to him. We simply draw attention to him and his glory—to the beauty we see everywhere we look, to the infinite power and wisdom we read about in the Bible, to the stunning grace and mercy we receive in his love for us. The breakthrough that exploded in front of me were these words from John Piper: "God is most glorified in us when we are most satisfied in him."[2] God begins to look like everything he already is *through* me and my life—his perfect holiness, his flawless justice, his unstoppable love—when he and his love begin to be everything *to* me. When our lives tell others *he* is our greatest treasure, he begins to look as great and glorious as he truly is. God made us to show *us* his glory, and by showing us more of himself, he planned to make us the happiest people who have ever lived. I learned that the bigger and more glorious God is in my heart, the bigger and more glorious he will be through my life, and the more I'll be what he made me to be.

What is God's will for your life (and for your future marriage)? "Whether you eat or drink, or whatever you do, do all *to the glory of God*" (1 Cor. 10:31). In absolutely everything you do—even down to how you drink Gatorade after you work out or sip your favorite drink at Starbucks—do it for the glory of God. What does that mean? Paul goes on to say that he seeks "to please everyone in everything . . . not seeking [his] own advantage, but that of many, *that they may be saved*" (1 Cor. 10:33). Drink and eat, work and play, date and marry in ways that strive to win the world for Jesus. Invite them into the overwhelming, life-changing love you've found. Whatever you do, do it to say something about what God has done for you and about how much he means to you.

Don't do anything just to do it, just to fit in and follow the world's script for your life. Let all of your life—your waiting, your dating, your wanting—be brought up into the purpose God had for you when he made you, weaving you together with love in your mother's womb (Ps. 139:13). Build your life on his love and make your purpose his glory.

An Awful Trade and Greater Love

But "all have sinned and fall short of the glory of God" (Rom. 3:23). We all fall short of his glory, and not just in our past but today and every day. You, me, and everyone you know, no exceptions. Paul says we "exchanged the glory of the immortal God for images resembling mortal man and birds and animals and creeping things" (Rom. 1:23). Instead of living to be an image of God, we take our eyes off him and let our hearts focus on something else. We trade the infinite worth of the unseen for a few minutes with things we can see. We are born into sin, and we live in love with our sin (Ps. 51:5; John 3:19). And "the wages of sin is death" (Rom. 6:23). Not a slap on the wrist, not some inconvenience in this life, not a little less from God. Death. Unbearable pain and agony away from God and his grace, and the pain never ends. We deserve *that* for disregarding God's love and his purpose for our lives, for rejecting the path to happiness he paved for us.

How has God responded to our sin—to trading his glory for our own, looking to marriage or money or anything else for life and happiness instead of to him? He "became flesh and dwelt among us, and we have seen his glory, glory as of the only Son from the Father, full of grace and truth" (John 1:14). In Jesus Christ, God came in all his glory to save those who had trashed his glory and to remake them into living, breathing, and believing images of his worth and beauty, again. You were made for glory, and you were *saved* for glory.

A Heaven without God

This landed on me for the first time that same year I decided to be a business major, and it changed my whole perspective on my dreams, my major, the possibility of marriage, and the rest of my life. I realized that the gospel was a story for me but that it was not a story *about* me. This good news—the news that rescued me from hell and promised me heaven—was not about God making me happy apart from him and his glory, but about satisfying me now and forever *with himself*. He loved me enough to give me himself. I highlighted this paragraph then, and I go back and read it once a year or so:

> Christ did not die to forgive sinners who go on treasuring anything above seeing and savoring God. And the people who would be happy in heaven if Christ were not there, will not be there. The gospel is not a way to get people to heaven; it is a way to get people to God.[3]

Why did God save you? Not just so that you could escape hell or relieve some shame and regret, not even so that you could get into heaven. God saved you *for God*. The Bible says God loved you, chose you, saved you, and made you his own "to the praise of his glorious grace" (Eph. 1:6). Paul goes on to say that the one who works *everything* in the world according to his will has set aside an infinite and everlasting inheritance *for you* "to the praise of his glory" (Eph. 1:12). "In him you also, when you heard the word of truth, the gospel of your salvation, and believed in him, were sealed with the promised Holy Spirit, who is the guarantee of our inheritance until we acquire possession of it, *to the praise of his glory*" (vv. 13–14). *Saved* to make God look glorious. *Blessed* to make God look satisfying. *Kept* to make God look worthy. And because he loves you.

His love for you is unlike any love you have ever known. You will never fully understand or grasp it. But by his grace and strength, you will know and feel more and more of it. Paul prays and asks "that you, being rooted and grounded *in love*, may have strength to comprehend with all the saints what is the breadth and length and height and depth, and to know the love of Christ that surpasses knowledge" (Eph. 3:17–19). You will spend forever exploring this love, discovering its breadth and length and height and depth. His purpose for you began before you were even born and lasts into eternity. God wanted to make you infinitely happy forever, centuries after your future marriage is a sweet but faint memory. Can you live now for the glory of a God who saves you and loves you like that?

2

Single, Satisfied, and Sent

For almost two years, I spent a couple hours a week with Will. Will volunteered at the food shelf where I worked part-time while I was still in graduate school. He was African-American and twice my age. He was the father of three daughters and already a grandfather. And Will was a recovering (and still struggling) alcoholic.

For two years I walked a few blocks from where I lived to a rehab center that specialized in alcohol dependency. It was not a Christian clinic, but they gave me permission to hold a Bible study once a week in one of their conference rooms for anyone who was interested. Not-yet-married me had plenty of time and energy to spare. I was twenty-two the first time I made that walk, praying as I made my way up 19th Avenue. A few times, there were four or five people, but usually there was only one, and sometimes no one showed. Each week I wandered the halls of the clinic trying to round up a few to come sit and read with me for an hour. Most of them were twenty or thirty years older than I. They usually greeted me with a warm smile and a friendly "Reverend."

One day I met Will. Will's grandmother had taught him the Bible, and she had taught him well enough that he remembered a verse here and there. Will came most weeks, even meeting me at the food shelf when he stopped his treatment at the clinic. Every week I walked the halls looking for more takers, but most weeks it was just me and Will, reading slowly through the Gospel of John. Some weeks he did better than others with his rehab, but I began to see his faith grow and come alive as we opened the Bible together.

Eventually I moved to another neighborhood and started going to another church. I didn't keep up with Will after that, but to this day I can't imagine a better way I could have spent all those Wednesday afternoons, alone with Will, telling him more about Jesus. Hardly anybody knew I had gone to the clinic each week, sometimes sitting there alone for fifteen or twenty minutes before giving up and walking home. But God taught me a lot about myself and about our mission in the world on those Wednesdays between 2:30 and 4:00 p.m. Most of all, he taught me that living for his glory is not about building the biggest ministry or winning the most people but about faithfully telling people about my King, wherever he leads me. In fact, his glory often shines even more brightly in the small, quiet, unseen things we do for him. In people like Will.

Authority, Clarity, and Urgency

We are saved to go out into the world—single or married—for the glory of our Jesus, to make him *known* as our Lord, Savior, and greatest treasure. Redemption is a lifesaving rescue, but it also involves a profound rewiring and repurposing. Conversion is about commission, not just salvation, because we're not saved to be saved, but saved to be sent. But how do we individually live out God's purpose for us in our everyday lives? With some of his very last words on earth, Jesus sent his disciples into the world to change the world:

All authority in heaven and on earth has been given to me. Go therefore and make disciples of all nations, baptizing them in the name of the Father and of the Son and of the Holy Spirit, teaching them to observe all that I have commanded you. And behold, I am with you always, to the end of the age. (Matt. 28:18–20)

We call it the *Great* Commission because of its authority, its clarity, and its urgency. If the president of the United States called you today and asked you to deliver a message to everyone on your block, would you do it? What if he was warning you about the deadly outbreak of some kind of rare and contagious disease in your city? And what if there were a series of simple but critical steps every person could do to avoid contamination (for example, avoid all seafood, drink Kombucha, and eat some Starburst)? The *president* chose to call you *with instructions* to save the hundred people on your block, *or they will die* (authority, clarity, and urgency).

As Christians, we have been charged with a life-and-death responsibility by one infinitely higher than the president of the United States. Jesus Christ—the Son of God, Wonderful Counselor, Almighty God, King of kings, Lord of lords—has given us a mission. *All* authority in heaven *and* on earth is his. And the mission for us is clear: "Go therefore and *make disciples of all nations, baptizing them* in the name of the Father and of the Son and of the Holy Spirit, *teaching them* to observe all that I have commanded you." And there's never been more at stake. At the end of their short life here on earth, some will hear, "Come, you who are blessed by my Father, inherit the kingdom prepared for you from the foundation of the world" (Matt. 25:34). Others will hear, "Depart from me, you cursed, into the eternal fire prepared for the devil and his angels" (Matt. 25:41). The world will only ever be saved by grace. But they have to hear about it first. Paul says the same thing in different words:

"Everyone who calls on the name of the Lord will be saved." How then will they call on him in whom they have not believed? And how are they to believe in him of whom they have never heard? And how are they to hear without someone preaching? And how are they to preach unless they are sent? (Rom. 10:13–15)

And yet the workers are so very few. Why? Because we treat the awesome authority of Jesus Christ like the authority of a middle-school gym teacher or a mall cop on a Segway. Because we treat the lifesaving, destiny-shaping news of the gospel as if it offered only some suggestions for a healthier and more successful life. Because we take the simple instruction to teach others what *Jesus says* and instead make it our Christian mission to be good neighbors, good employees, and, Lord willing, good spouses and parents one day. As David Platt says, "We live decent lives in decent homes with decent jobs and decent families as decent citizens."[4] We strip the gospel and the Bible of its authority, its clarity, and its urgency to make it fit into our small, comfortable American dreams and priorities and put off getting more serious about Christianity until we get married and start a family. We love Jesus, accept him as Lord, and read his words—and then we get distracted and drag our feet. Instead of doing what we're told, we do what comes naturally and feels comfortable. Instead of following Jesus, we fit in. We delegate the mission to people in full-time Christian ministry and look for free time to do some service project in the name of Jesus.

Satan Is after You

We have an enemy in this work. Satan, in and through the world around us, will do everything possible to distract us and keep us from doing what God saved us and sent us to do, convincing us to waste our lives on lesser things. You need to know that there are some unique dangers in singleness—especially in unwanted singleness. He loves to deceive and discourage single people in the church and derail our devotion and ministry. He convinces us we're not gifted or that our gifts can't be used for ministry. He isolates us from the people around us—those who can encourage and challenge us in our walk with Christ, *and* those who need us in their lives. He distracts us, persuading us to pour ourselves into school, or work, or entertainment. But God intends to use you, your faith, your time, and your singleness in radical ways right now, as you are. You don't have to wait to get to the most important work you'll ever do.

Paul—an umarried man who wrote most of the New Testament—writes, "Now as a concession, not a command, I say this. I wish that all were as I myself am. But each has his own gift from God, one of one kind and one of another. To the unmarried and the widows I say that it is good for them to remain single, as I am" (1 Cor. 7:6–8). You might come away from reading 1 Corinthians 7 with two categories in mind: those who will live, serve, and die single and those who must marry. Paul sings singleness's praises, listing the spiritual benefits of being spouse-free. The single life can be (relatively) free from relational anxieties (v. 32) and worldly distractions (v. 33) and wide open for worship, devotion, and ministry (v. 35). So, Paul concludes, skip the ceremony, literally, and enjoy "your undivided devotion to the Lord."

Most say, "More power to you, Paul . . . but I'm getting married." I did. Maybe temptation overwhelms us, and we need a God-honoring way to satisfy that longing (v. 2). Maybe it's abundantly clear that we need a helper to carry out God's call on our life (or it's abundantly clear to others that we do). Maybe we want to have kids and realize that we need some help with that. Maybe we just have a deep, undeniable desire for a loving, committed companion. While it may seem like there are two categories, we quickly learn in application that there are really three:

the single, the married, and the not yet married. After all, as any single person knows, a desire for marriage does not a marriage make. Some do not feel any discernible call to singleness but are still single. These not-yet-married men and women face their own unique questions, challenges, and temptations. Satan waits in our waiting to discourage us and to make us feel immature or incomplete—like a junior varsity Christian. But if Jesus Christ died to save you and sent his Spirit to live in you, there's nothing junior varsity about you at all. And nothing in marriage is necessary for a meaningful and fruitful Christian life. Otherwise, Paul (and Jesus) just drew short straws.

All Dressed Up and Everywhere to Go

Perhaps the greatest temptation in singleness is to assume marriage will meet our unmet needs, solve our weaknesses, organize our lives, and unleash our gifts. Far from the solution, Paul makes marriage out to be a kind of problematic Plan B for Christian life and ministry. Marry if you must, but be warned that following Jesus is not easier when you join yourself to another sinner in a fallen world. While marriage may bring joy, help, and relief in certain areas, it immediately multiplies our distractions, because we're responsible for this other person, his or her needs, dreams, and growth. It's a high calling and a good calling but a demanding one that will keep us from all kinds of other good things.

If God leads you to marry, you may never again know a time like the one you're in right now. A season of singleness is not the minor leagues of marriage. It has the potential to be a unique period of undivided devotion to Christ and undistracted ministry to others. With the Spirit in you and the calendar clear, God has given you the means to make a lasting difference for his kingdom. You're all dressed up, having every spiritual blessing in the heavenly places (Eph. 1:3), with literally everywhere to go.

But where do I go, and what do I do? I can't answer that for everyone, but following are five lessons that may help you change the world (or at least your little piece of it) while you're not yet married. With God's help and leading, you have the freedom to invest yourself, your time, your resources, your youth, and your flexibility in relationships, ministries, and causes that can bear unbelievable fruit—to live single, satisfied, and sent.

1. Remember that true greatness will often look like weakness.

When Jesus finally explained to his disciples just what kind of king he was—just what it meant to be truly, deeply, lastingly *great*—he said to them, "The Son of Man is going to be delivered into the hands of men, and they will kill him. And when he is killed, after three days he will rise" (Mark 9:31). How did they respond? They walked away arguing over which one of them was the greatest— the chief among the otherwise forgettable fishermen (Mark 9:34). Instead of hearing Jesus talk about his death and redefining greatness in terms of sacrifice—in terms of coming in last for the sake of love—they fought to be first. According to Jesus, the greatest won't look all that great. In fact, true greatness will often look like weakness, surrender, defeat, and even death.

Most of the time, instead of pursuing greatness through sacrifice, I find myself expecting God to make life a little more comfortable, or relationships a little easier, or ministry a little more fruitful, or affirmation a little more regular. But he says, instead, "Whoever would be great among you must be your servant, and whoever would be first among you must be slave of all" (Mark 10:43–44). Servants in this life will rule the next. Slaves in this life will be kings forever. True greatness isn't the kind that appears in bold letters on our favorite website. No, it shows up in the details of other people's lives, in lives like Will's. If we aspire to be great, we need to give ourselves to the small, mundane, easily overlooked needs around us.

2. Notice the people God has already put around you.

God has put you on the planet and in your neighborhood so that you and all the people in your life might seek *him*. That's God's mission statement for your campus, your apartment building, your block—wherever you live, study, or work. Paul says that God "made from one man every nation of mankind to live on all the face of the earth, having determined allotted periods and the boundaries of their dwelling place, *that they should seek God*, and perhaps feel their way toward him and find him" (Acts 17:26–27).

God has determined our dwelling place today—*our* distinct home, in *our* particular neighborhood, in *our* specific city—*so that* we would seek him and help others do the same. It's not beyond God to use us to convert someone through a random, brief interaction with a stranger at the gym or a coffee shop. But friendships are the front lines of disciple making, and friendship requires some shared interest, hobby, or space—a place where paths cross. Even the always-traveling apostle Paul found time for that kind of relational, life-on-life evangelism and discipleship (1 Thess. 2:8). I led a Bible study at that particular clinic because it was three blocks from where I lived. Notice the people God has put in your life, however he has put them in your life, and do whatever you can to encourage them to seek Jesus.

3. Practice selflessness while you're still single.

"Do nothing from selfish ambition or conceit, but in humility count others more significant than yourselves. Let each of you look not only to his own interests, but also to the interests of others" (Phil. 2:3–4). That will only get harder in marriage, so practice now. We should think of a few people or families for whom we could lay down our single life. No one is expecting you to care for and provide for others right now—no one, that is, except for God. Let's be mindful of the needs of others, especially those in the church, and consider contributing. It could be money or food, or just time and energy. Maybe *especially* time and energy.

Regardless of our paycheck, we have been given much. We should spend it wisely and liberally on the needs of others. Financially, you're supporting just one person. Sure, save modestly for days when you'll need more, but while you wait, look for ways to provide for others. While you're not buying groceries for five, dinner for two, or endless diapers, budget to bless, and develop attitudes and habits of sacrifice for others. Those habits will serve your future spouse immensely and make Jesus shine beautifully to those around you in the meantime.

4. Say yes to the spontaneous.

It's just a fact—marriage murders spontaneity, not entirely but massively. One of your greatest spiritual gifts as a single person is your *yes*. Yes to a random phone conversation. Yes to coffee. Yes to help with the move. Yes to stepping in when someone's sick. Yes to a late-night movie or the special event downtown. You have the unbelievable freedom to say yes when married people can't even ask the question. When the spouse doesn't exist yet, you cannot hurt him or her with the selfless, impulsive decisions you make to serve others. If you get married, you will not always have the same freedom. Be willing to say yes and be a blessing to others, even when you don't always feel like it.

5. Do radical, time-consuming things for God.

Just as you are free to say yes to spontaneous things, you're also able to say yes to things that require more of you than a married person can afford. Dream bigger, more costly dreams. Start a daily prayer meeting or some regular outreach. Commit to mentor and disciple several men or women younger than you. Organize a new Christ-centered community service project. Do all of the above. You'd be surprised, with God's Spirit in you and a resolve to spend your singleness well, how much you and your not-yet-married friends are truly capable of, especially when you dream and work together. Be radical but not reckless. The idea is *not* to spread yourself dangerously thin, so make decisions prayerfully and in community with people who love you and can tell you no.

I led the Bible study at the rehab center down the street. While I was not yet married, I also mentored high school students through Young Life and started a small group among post-college men and women at our church. I went on missions trips to the Dominican Republic, India, and Ethiopia. I worked with others to start an ESL class and a ministry to refugees living near our church. Living for God's glory this year may look like teaching with a Christian school in South Korea for a year, and it may look like serving in Sunday school with two or three students with significant mental disabilities. We have a friend doing each, and God looks as beautiful as ever in both. How could you use your gifts to do something radical or time-consuming to tell others about Jesus?

Sent by God into a World of Distraction

Our mission is clear, but we still miss it sometimes. We're so distracted by everything else there is to see and do. Paul may have been right about the single person's freedom from anxieties and distractions in marriage, but in an iPhone, iPad, whatever iWant world, we never have trouble finding our share of diversions. In fact, if you're like me, you crave diversion and tend to default there, whether it's watching SportsCenter or Hulu, working out, fancy eating, scrolling social media, or conquering the latest video game. We might call it resting, but too often it looks, smells, and sounds a lot like we're wasting our singleness—at least it did for me sometimes. Everything just mentioned can be done for God's glory, *and* it all can be a dangerous distraction from it. If we deny the latter, we may need to put down the smartphone, controller, or treadmill. In the next chapter, we'll look at these distractions—things God has made to give us more joy in him but that sadly, instead, often lead us away from him and the important work he's given us.

3

Undivided and Undistracted

The not yet married today live in the most technologically advanced generation in history. That means we also live in the most connected generation and therefore likely the most distracted one. Distraction has always threatened faith in Jesus—long before cable television, the first iPhone, and Candy Crush. Jesus said that some will hear the word of God, "but as they go on their way they are choked by the cares and riches and pleasures of life, and their fruit does not mature" (Luke 8:14). Still today, every distraction—good or bad—could probably be given one of those three labels: cares, riches, or pleasures. The three are different, but Jesus warned us that each has the power to distract us from him, blind us to his worth, and deafen us to his Word. In that way, distractions can decide our destinies.

As Christians, we are the happy, hope-filled, and strange people who "look not to the things that are seen but to the things that are unseen. For the things that are seen are transient, but the things that are unseen are eternal" (2 Cor. 4:18). But there's just so much to see in this world! Another movie, another football game, another fashion trend, another app. All the cares, riches, and pleasures make it easy to forget the unseen and to settle for far less. The things that distract us are not necessarily bad in themselves. If God is our treasure, his glory our mission, and his Word our guide, we can enjoy all his gifts to the full. But the gifts become destructive when they distract us from him. God says, "My people have committed two evils: they have forsaken me, the fountain of living waters, and hewed out cisterns for themselves, broken cisterns that can hold no water" (Jer. 2:13). We skip the fountain and hit up the vending machine instead. We take things God has given us to point us to him, and we try to make them hold the living water only he can carry for us. We turn gifts into gods. And as the world watches our life—how we spend our free time, what we talk about, where we spend our money—they will know where our heart lives (Matt. 6:21). God will too.

The problem with so many of us today is that we have close to no anxiety about spiritual realities and endless anxiety about the things of this world. We attend church weekly, maybe even join a small group, but we don't lose any sleep over Christianity. It doesn't cost us much at all. We pray for fifteen seconds before most meals but don't know how to talk to God for much longer than that. We spend a few minutes in the Bible here and there but nowhere near as much time as we spend browsing our social media feeds. We have all the time in the world for the things that will not last and so very little time for the things that last forever.

I say "we," not "you." I'm a sports fan—Reds and Bengals (yes, there are a few Cincinnati fans out there). My wife and I have our favorite TV shows. We love trying new restaurants, especially sushi and Thai food. I love to read, and she loves pinning things on Pinterest to cook or put up around our house. You can find me on social media. All these things are filled with potential to help me make much of God as the creative and generous Father who loves giving his kids good things. And all are pulsing with the power to draw my attention and affection away from God and his purpose for me. Married or unmarried, distractions have the ability to destroy us.

Saying "I Do" to Distractions

Marriage is very good—in the Bible and from experience—but it does demand a lot of you. Marriage will not complete you (at least not in the way most people imagine); it will divide you. Paul loved marriage and what a Christian marriage says to the world (Eph. 5:22–27, 32), but he also knew what love like that costs. He knew that intimacy in a covenant comes with great responsibility. The blessings—and they are many—come with burdens to bear.

Paul says, "Those who marry will have worldly troubles, and I would spare you that" (1 Cor. 7:28). He uses the same word for "worldly troubles" elsewhere to describe poverty (2 Cor. 8:2), persecution (1 Thess. 1:6), and even the cross (Col. 1:24). That doesn't mean marriage isn't filled with incredible joy. All of Paul's deepest joys came through sacrifice and suffering (Rom. 5:3–5). Like everything difficult done for Christ, marriage strengthens us to endure in faith, refines and purifies our character, reinforces the hope we have in our Redeemer, and reminds us of the flood of God's love that's been poured into hearts and lives.

So why does Paul encourage people to think twice before getting married? He says, "I want you to be free from anxieties. The unmarried man is anxious about the things of the Lord, how to please the Lord. But the married man is anxious about worldly things, how to please his wife, and his interests are divided" (1 Cor. 7:32–34). Anxiety in marriage is not ungodly or unnecessary. In fact, anxiety is critical to having a healthy marriage that makes much of Jesus. If a husband is not anxious for his wife, or a wife has no concern for her husband, the marriage might survive, but it cannot be healthy. We have to feel a constant responsibility for one another, being attentive to each other's needs—daily (and joyfully) being distracted with one another.

The distractions are not (necessarily) burdensome, but they're real. Paul does the simple math for married people: some of the time and energy and attention you spend caring for your spouse cannot also be spent on Jesus and others. It doesn't mean you won't find creative and meaningful ways to pursue Christ and do ministry *together*. You will, and you should. It does mean you will have to spend lots of time focused on your spouse's needs and not on your personal devotion to the Lord or on using your gifts to fulfill the Great Commission. In marriage, you will see and experience the gospel in ways you never have before, *and* you will probably have fewer opportunities to pray, read, and serve than you did while you were single. It's a good trade—I *love* being married—but it's a real trade.

Paul so believed in the potential of singleness that he even encouraged widows to remain single. He says a little later, "A wife is bound to her husband as long as he lives. But if her husband dies, she is free to be married to whom she wishes, only in the Lord. Yet in my judgment she is happier if she remains as she is" (1 Cor. 7:39–40). Think about that for a minute—a thirty- or forty- or fifty-year-old woman left alone, maybe with children, no husband to provide for or protect her. Paul says *even she* might be better off not marrying. He could only say that because of how focused he was on the next life and on making this life count for that one. His conclusion in all of this? "So then he who marries his betrothed does *well*, and he who refrains from marriage will do even *better*" (1 Cor. 7:38). Marriage is very good. Singleness may be even better. Are your views of Jesus, heaven, and hell big enough to believe that?

Life Is Short

Most will strive just to survive singleness and wait to get serious about Jesus and his mission later, when things have settled down in life. A brave few of us will develop not-yet-married habits of knowing him deeply and sharing him freely, likely far beyond what we would be able to do after our wedding day. Singleness has the potential to be a garden—or a gym, or a kitchen, or a school—for undistracted devotion to Jesus unlike any other season of our lives. To believe that, we need to learn some things about this life. Those who live for God's glory—who live for the next life in this one—*will* feel a persistent, even painful urgency.

The work we have to do, in our own hearts and for the sake of the lost, is the most important work that's ever been done in history. And there isn't much time. John writes, "The world is passing away along with its desires, but whoever does the will of God abides forever" (1 John 2:17). Unlike you and heaven, earth is expiring, and relatively quickly. In the light of eternity, everything around you that looks so strong, real, and entertaining will be gone before we know it. This world—its promises, its experiences, its priorities—are not the best investment of our energy and anxiety.

Life is short. You and everyone around you will live, on average, a little more than seventy years. That will feel like less than a bathroom break compared with the eternity ahead of us. Everything in the world is teaching you to stretch out every moment as long as possible, to soak up every last drop from your time here on earth. But you weren't made for this, and you won't be here long. We have to stop believing the lie that everything we have here is all we have, and start thinking of everything we have here as something to invest in what's to come. If the whole world passed away today, would we love what's left? We develop those spiritual muscles now by saying, with everything we have and do now, that Jesus is our greatest treasure. Life is short, and everything we have and see here is passing away. Everything but Jesus.

Heaven and Hell

We also have to be reminded that Jesus really is coming back. This is not like Saint Nicholas coming again next December. The crucified, risen, and reigning Jesus will return, and soon. He said so before he died: "They will see the Son of Man coming on the clouds of heaven with power and great glory" (Matt. 24:30). Do you really expect Jesus to come back, rescue you out of this world, and make all things new again? Do you *want* him to come back? He will come on that day "to be glorified in his saints, and to be marveled at among all who have believed" (2 Thess. 1:10). He will appear to all who have believed, and he will be stunningly beautiful, compelling, and satisfying. We'll never need to look at anything else ever again. We will see and enjoy lots of other things in the new heavens and the new earth, but we won't need to. He'll be enough for us forever.

But what about for those who have *not* believed? Just one verse earlier Paul says God will inflict "vengeance on those who do not know God and on those who do not obey the gospel of our Lord Jesus. They will suffer the punishment of eternal destruction, away from the presence of the Lord and from the glory of his might" (2 Thess. 1:8–9). Life is short, and hell is real. Some will see God and never need again. Others will live their whole life and never know God, some of them being exposed to the gospel and rejecting it and others never even hearing the name of Jesus. All of them lost and condemned because of their sin against God. I'm ashamed to say that my life—my priorities, my conversations, my boldness—have not always said to others that heaven and hell are real. We should be passionate, persistent, and *anxious* for them to see that he's better than anything this world offers and that living for anything else only leads to awful, conscious, never-ending pain and punishment.

Life is short, Jesus is coming, and heaven and hell are real. Simple, weighty truths like these are our weapons in the war against distraction. Those whose hearts are being shaped like God's will have a sense of urgency in this life and a wariness of distractions that keep them and others from enjoying more of God forever. We should be anxious about the spiritual realities under everything happening in our life and relationships, because there is so much at stake. We should feel the weight of our lost planet and the urgency of our few days on it.

The World Will Not Care for You

The cares of the world can grab our attention and affection for a moment, but they cannot satisfy us for long—here today, gone in seconds. Most of the time, we don't worry about how much time we give it because it all seems so harmless—in one ear, and out the other, pushed further and further down our Facebook feed. Jesus says these kinds of distractions are more dangerous than we realize. They feed us news—sports scores, online deals, controversy, analysis, gossip—until we can't live without them. He warned us that some will hear the Word and like what they hear, "but the cares of the world and the deceitfulness of riches and the desires for other things enter in and choke the word, and it proves unfruitful" (Mark 4:19). What does he mean by "choke"? A few verses earlier he says, "Seed fell among thorns, and the thorns grew up and choked it, and it yielded no grain" (Mark 4:7). The world is filled with thorns trying to cover up, crowd out, and *choke* God's Word from your heart. Do you feel that throughout your week? Do you feel the constant battle for your attention and affection?

The call is not to think about Jesus and *only* Jesus all the time. God wants us to enjoy every gift for his glory, and he gives us lots of gifts besides his Son. Paul asks, "He who did not spare his own Son but gave him up for us all, how will he not also with him graciously give us all things?" (Rom. 8:32). In Jesus, we have already been promised *all* things. That means we're free not to have to know, or own, or experience everything in our seventy or eighty years here. We're going to get it all (1 Cor. 3:21–23). Why are we so anxious, then, about the cares of this life—what we will wear, how many followers we have, how much we make, what he said about her or she said about him? We ought to be painfully anxious and passionate about spiritual realities—about Jesus, heaven, and hell. We do *not* need to be so anxious about everything else. That kind of anxiety will only weigh us down and make us ineffective in life (Prov. 12:25).

Our Window into the World

What is the main window today into the cares of this world? You probably carry it in your pocket or purse. Our smartphones are instruments of mass distraction. They've been engineered—decades now of testing and marketing—to distract us. By God's grace, our devices can be wielded for spreading the gospel and God's Word through new and popular mediums to millions all over the world. I write for desiringGod.org, a website that leverages technology to help people be happy *in Jesus* (and not in technology).

Our phones can also distract us to death and keep us from ever putting them down. I've been the offender too often in our home. Satan presents a host of lies to keep us attached to our phones, and therefore to the cares of this world—a kind of twisted spiritual "upgrade" from the corded phone. Phones were once attached to walls; now we're attached to them. Two lies are especially compelling and sum up a lot of the others. Gaining freedom from our phones requires being liberated from lies like these that bind the technology to us like links in a cold, steel chain.

Lie 1: The world needs me.

For some of us, a savior complex tethers us to our phones. We're afraid something will happen and someone will need us—and only us—immediately. What could they possibly do if we weren't available? Well, probably whatever they did for thousands of years before the telephone existed, or for a couple hundred more while it was anchored to the wall. Or more likely, and yet strangely unthinkable to a me-centered generation, they'll just call some-one else.

The world doesn't need me. God has governed, preserved, and prospered the world without me for most of history—thousands and thousands of years. If I suddenly died tomorrow, there would undoubtedly be significant pain, loss, and change for a few, but the world would survive, move forward, and be just fine. The omniscient and omnipotent God is still in control and utterly com-mitted to fulfilling his work everywhere on the planet. He will take care of every detail with perfect love, perfect timing, and unlimited power. And he'll be especially and graciously attentive when it comes to protecting and providing for those who love him (Matt. 6:26–30).

Lie 2: I need the world.

We have a need to be needed. We love the idea that someone might text or call or tweet to get our attention. We don't want to miss that moment when someone else thought of us. Alert after alert reassures us we're important and loved—even if the affection is often shallow, superficial, and short-lived. Our smartphones make us feel needed, and they give us control, or at least the illusion of control. We decide when to click, what apps to add, and whom to engage. Face-to-face relationships aren't as convenient as Face-book friends or Snapchat followers. But those friendships and re-lationships are the front lines of faithfulness, and the opportunities with the greatest potential for lasting impact.

Like a desperate, sleep-deprived reporter, we check our sources every few minutes, looking for the next headline—sports, eating, politics, and pop culture. We work hard to be in the know but end up knowing everything about nothing. Tragically, we know the latest trends on Twitter, the funniest videos on YouTube, and the Instagrammed milestones of others' infants, but we have a harder time answering questions about the people actually living in our lives. As believers in Jesus and the gospel, our identity is never in how much we're needed in this life, or in what we control, or in how much we know. Our life is measured by the life that was given for us, by the price that was paid to secure and satisfy us forever (1 Cor. 6:20). We were made and saved not to be loved by social media—by whatever distractions bind us to our phone—but by the almighty God of holiness and mercy.

Cast Every Care on Him

This almighty God of holiness and mercy is not just a judge or a king, but he's a dad. He watches over and loves you as one of his own sons or daughters. You have an all-wise and all-powerful Father in heaven, who knows everything you need and promises to deliver it precisely when you need it. Jesus says:

> Therefore I tell you, *do not be anxious* about your life, what you will eat or what you will drink, nor about your body, what you will put on. . . . Your heavenly Father knows that you need them all. But seek first the kingdom of God and his righteousness, and all these things will be added to you. (Matt. 6:25, 32–33)

You do not need to be anxious about—distracted by—food, or drink, or clothing, or any of your circumstances in this life. You are held by your heavenly Father. He knows everything about you, down to what socks you will wear tomorrow and what you will drink with lunch. He's aware of everything you need, he has everything at his disposal, and he loves you. Cast your anxieties (and your distractions) onto him, "because he cares for you" (1 Pet. 5:7). Let the love he has shown you in Christ free you from everything else that demands your attention.

4

Love the Life You Never Wanted

Singleness brings its own suffering, a kind of misery many married people simply don't understand anymore. I wonder what the hardest days are for you? Maybe it's been a breakup (or several). Or maybe it's been that nothing's ever gotten that far. There's never been a real boyfriend or girlfriend who *might* break up with you. Maybe you gave up and started experimenting sexually—in relationships or online—looking for love, pleasure, and control, and instead finding shame, regret, and slavery. Maybe you've wanted to be a mom or a dad since you were old enough to know what one was. You've dreamed and dreamed about having little boys and girls of your own. You love your friends' kids, but bitterness creeps in sometimes. Maybe you're just longing for friendship or companionship, someone to laugh and cry with. More people probably want to be married because of loneliness than because of sex and children combined. That's my guess anyway. Maybe married people have made a few too many insensitive comments, encouraging you to enjoy "dating Jesus," or reminding you how great it is to wait, or trying to hook you up with their uncle's daughter's friend's sister. Maybe it has nothing to do with dating or marriage for you. Maybe it's your parents' relationship or divorce, or losing someone you loved too soon, or getting diagnosed with a life-threatening or life-altering condition or disease. Like everyone else, every not-yet-married person will experience pain, but pain will be magnified in some ways by singleness.

Breakups are often the lowest valleys and highest hurdles in the early days of the not-yet-married life. At least they were in mine. I remember those days and those conversations more vividly than any of the best days in dating. Every breakup is hard, but some hurt more than others. One girl and I had dated for a long time, probably close to a year. We had made all kinds of memories, knew each other's families well, and had done a lot of ministry together. It all felt so right and so sure. What could possibly go wrong?

Well, she broke up with me. I knew things weren't always great, that I hadn't always led her well in the relationship, and that there were points of real concern and disagreement between us, but I didn't think it would come to *this*. I didn't think she'd actually leave. Then she did. And she told me very clearly that we'd never date again. "Friends, nothing more." I was devastated at the time. I didn't even think about dating anyone for a whole year. That might be nothing to you (and it should be), but for me, at that point in my life, it was an eternity. I'd love to say it was because I was refocusing my heart on Jesus (and that did happen throughout that year), but really I was just hoping she would come back to me. I was consumed by the rejection, by my desire for marriage, and by the loneliness I felt without her.

Well, she did come back. Right when I began to lose hope that we'd ever get back together, she texted and wanted to meet. "We need to talk." We met that night, and through lots of tears she told me that she wanted to get back together. All my dreams suddenly came true. I had waited, with sackcloth and ashes, and God had finally rewarded me. Right? We dated for another year or so, and the same issues came up again, and it was clear to most people (including her), that we should not be pursuing marriage together. My parents tried to discourage me, and even my friends expressed reservations. But I still believed we were going to get married, that we could simply overlook the issues, and that we'd make it through. I guess I had believed that about every relationship, even back to when I was thirteen or fourteen. *Of course we're going to get married. Why would we ever break up?* Well, against all my experience, and against everything God had taught me, and against all the yellow flags in our relationship, I blindly and stubbornly believed again.

But right when I foolishly thought we were ready to get engaged, she broke up with me—again. This time, for good. And she was right. Naïve and immature, I had fallen more in love with getting married than I had ever actually loved her. And my love affair with marriage left me confused, hurting, and despairing without a girlfriend. The pain I felt revealed what I loved. The despair uncovered what I believed—about God, about myself, and about marriage. My misery exposed my idolatry. My suffering in singleness, most of it impatiently self-inflicted, taught me to reorder my loves and to live (and date) differently.

Satan Hunts among the Hurting

Mountain lions detect vulnerabilities in their prey and attack the weakest—the young, the sick, the injured. It's how the mountain lion lives, following the scent of suffering and feasting on whatever he finds. The enemy of our hope and happiness hunts with a mountain lion's instinct, with a coldhearted and ruthless hunger for disappointed or hurting. "The devil prowls around like a roaring lion, seeking someone to devour" (1 Pet. 5:8). And because he's clever, he spends a lot of his time among the disappointed and afflicted. He lies in wait with lies, wanting to consume the fragile, the vulnerable, and the lonely. Singleness may have felt like that to you at times.

Our pain and suffering in this life reminds us we're at war. While God promises to work all things for the good of those who love him (Rom. 8:28), Satan prowls around trying to corrupt those same things and lace them with lies (Rev. 12:9). The painful moments in life—however those pains come—are the ones in which we're most likely to question God and go our own way, trusting ourselves more than God and trying to take control of our lives, again. Satan says to us, *God doesn't care about the pain you're going through. God isn't able to do anything about it, anyway. The distress, the misery, the adversity will never end.* But all the hard things in life that might tempt us to doubt God and his goodness are meant by God to lead us *to him.* God is warning us through pain that a powerful, compelling, and creative enemy wants to kill us and blind us to God's sovereign love for us. When we are disappointed or afflicted, God is calling us to war. He is lovingly and violently shaking us out of our complacency and entitlement to awaken us to the realities of life deeper and more important than our circumstances.

Cast Your Cares on Him

Peter knew what it felt like for Satan to pounce on him in difficult circumstances, to find himself suddenly gasping and drowning in temptation, to lack the strength to fight, and to feel totally alone. He abandoned and denied Jesus on the night he died—not once, but three times (Luke 22:60). Like a wounded infant deer pitifully trying to escape a predator, the once confident and strong Peter became the defenseless prey.

But before Jesus hung on the cross, he had prayed for Peter, that his faith would not fail and that his ministry would rise again from the ashes of fear and defeat (Luke 22:31–32). The same Peter who cowered in fear before the little servant girl, denying he'd ever known Jesus (Luke 22:56), was later courageously crucified for his faith. And before he boldly died to tell the world about his love for Jesus, he wrote a letter to suffering Christians everywhere and for all of time, even to today. He says to the hurting ones, "Humble yourselves, therefore, under the mighty hand of God so that at the proper time he may exalt you, casting all your anxieties on him, because he cares for you" (1 Pet. 5:6–7). Your present suffering will only be for a little while (1 Pet. 1:6), even if it's for the rest of your earthly life. And soon, God will lift ("exalt") you out of these difficult circumstances and into his safe and satisfying presence forever, away from everything you feared and suffered in this life (cf. Rom. 8:16–18; James 4:10). He will heal every wound, make up for every loss, and wipe away every tear (Rev. 21:4). In the place of our broken and painful experiences here on earth will be a never-ending well of the greatest joy we've ever known or tasted (Ps. 16:11). Peter had learned that Satan loves to hunt among the hurting, but he also learned that God arms us to fight well, even in pain and weakness. God plants invincible truths in our vulnerable hearts and then guards our faith with his infinite power (1 Pet. 1:4–5).

Ten Promises for Every Pain

We are at war, but we are not alone—even while we are not yet married. God is with us, and he cares for us. Before Jesus left the earth, as he commissioned his disciples to go into a dark world with the hope of the gospel, he said to them (and to us), "I am with you always, to the end of the age" (Matt. 28:20). And Peter promises even more company: "Resist [the Devil], firm in your faith, knowing that the same kinds of suffering are being experienced *by your brotherhood throughout the world*" (1 Pet. 5:9). You may not *know* someone in your immediate context suffering the same things as you, but you are not alone among Christians in the world and in history. God has cared for them, and he wants you to know he will care for you too. God's infinite wealth and power will meet and provide for God's weak and suffering people with God's relentless compassion and care *when* they are clinging together to God's Word, especially to his promises. But to cling to them, we have to know them. Here are ten promises from God for every pain, disappointment, and fear you and your friends face.

1. Knowing Jesus outweighs everything you could have or lose in this life.

> I count everything as loss because of the surpassing worth of knowing Christ Jesus my Lord. For his sake I have suffered the loss of all things and count them as rubbish, in order that I may gain Christ and be found in him. (Phil. 3:8–9)

2. Every trial is helping to prove the genuineness of your faith and joy.

> In this you rejoice, though now for a little while, if necessary, you have been grieved by various trials, so that the tested genuineness of your faith—more precious than gold that perishes though it is tested by fire—may be found to result in praise and glory and honor at the revelation of Jesus Christ. (1 Pet. 1:6–7)

3. All your pain is preparing you to care for others in pain.

> Blessed be the God . . . of all comfort, who comforts us in all our affliction, so that we may be able to comfort those who are in any affliction, with the comfort with which we ourselves are comforted by God. (2 Cor. 1:3–4)

4. Over time, suffering will fuel, not hurt, your hope and joy.

> We rejoice in our sufferings, knowing that suffering produces endurance, and endurance produces character, and character produces hope, and hope does not put us to shame, because God's love has been poured into our hearts. (Rom. 5:3–5)

5. *No suffering can steal what Jesus bought for you.*

You joyfully accepted the plundering of your property, since you knew that you yourselves had a better possession and an abiding one. (Heb. 10:34)

6. *Jesus never gets tired of caring for the tired.*

Come to me, all who labor and are heavy laden, and I will give you rest. Take my yoke upon you, and learn from me, for I am gentle and lowly in heart, and you will find rest for your souls. For my yoke is easy, and my burden is light. (Matt. 11:28–30)

7. *Suffering will give you faith and strength to endure to the end.*

Count it all joy, my brothers, when you meet trials of various kinds, for you know that the testing of your faith produces steadfastness. And let steadfastness have its full effect, that you may be perfect and complete, lacking in nothing. (James 1:2–4)

8. *God will pour out his infinite riches to meet your daily needs.*

My God will supply every need of yours according to his riches in glory in Christ Jesus. (Phil. 4:19)

9. *Not one ounce of your pain is meaningless but is producing glory for you.*

So we do not lose heart. Though our outer self is wasting away, our inner self is being renewed day by day. For this light momentary affliction is preparing for us an eternal weight of glory beyond all comparison. (2 Cor. 4:16–17)

10. *All of your suffering will end one day, down to the very last tear.*

He will wipe away every tear from their eyes, and death shall be no more, neither shall there be mourning, nor crying, nor pain anymore. (Rev. 21:4)

God wrote a book to comfort us in all our pain and to help us overcome all of our inevitable ignorance and insensitivity in trying to care for others in pain. As we receive God's words for us, even in the hardest things, we listen to the Creator of the world—the one who designed every inch of our bodies and authored every second of our story, including our pain. The God who speaks into all our pain through the Bible is the artist who painted all the brightest lights and all the darkest shadows into our lives. He knows our pain perfectly, and if we'll trust him and receive his words of hope, he promises good for us in whatever we're facing or suffering.

Sorrowful, Yet Always Rejoicing

So what does faith and humility look like in the midst of hardship and heartbreak? "Humble yourselves . . . casting all your anxieties on him [and all his promises], because he cares for you" (1 Pet. 5:6–7). Instead of defiantly hurling our affliction back at God with bitterness or fear, humility hands every anxiety back to him with affection and confidence. Humility refuses to treat God like an incompetent or unsympathetic boss, but comes to him, even in the sufferings of singleness, as to a compassionate and invested Father. Jesus says, "Look at the birds of the air: they neither sow nor reap nor gather into barns, and yet your heavenly Father feeds them. Are you not of more value than they?" (Matt. 6:26). If we truly believed that the God who created all things, having absolutely everything at his disposal, cares for us like a father, we would not resist him and his will as we do, even when life gets hard or we have to wait longer than we expected. "As servants of God we commend ourselves in every way: by great endurance, in afflictions, hardships, calamities, beatings, imprisonments, riots, labors, sleepless nights, hunger"— by years of singleness—"as sorrowful, *yet always rejoicing*; as poor, yet making many rich; as having nothing, yet possessing everything" (2 Cor. 6:4–10).

We follow Jesus, "who for the joy that was set before him endured the cross" (Heb. 12:2)—"he *humbled* himself by becoming obedient to the point of death" (Phil. 2:8). He suffered everything knowing the happiness of being held *by* heaven and *for* heaven. Will we find hope and strength in him to do the same? The high King of the universe was also the low and suffering servant. "He was despised and rejected by men; a man of sorrows and acquainted with grief; and as one from whom men hide their faces he was despised, and we esteemed him not" (Isa. 53:3). Our Savior experienced the darkest, most intense pain and loneliness. Why? "He was pierced for our transgressions; he was crushed for our iniquities; upon him was the chastisement that brought us peace, and with his wounds we are healed" (v. 5). With his eyes fixed on the reward, and filled with joy, he suffered *anything* to give us hope in our suffering. Jesus can sympathize with us and carry us through anything we face, for however long we face it, if we'll trust him and walk with him.

Disappointments and Unfulfilled Dreams

The pain of disappointment we feel in the not-yet-married life falls from trees filled with our expectations. Our dreams grow and get more beautiful over years and years in our young imaginations, and then reality reaps a harvest, almost indiscriminately plucking fruit that we want to taste for ourselves. I felt that way, anyway, after years of wanting marriage. We tend to define our life based on our perception of our progress. Am I where I thought I would be at this age? Have I achieved what I thought I would? Are my dreams more or less real today?

Our plans and dreams can become idols. Marriage is a good gift and a terrible god. Most of my grief in my teenage years and even into my twenties came from giving more of my heart to my future marriage than to God. It's easy to anchor our hope and happiness in a wife or husband and to define our growth, maturity, and worth by our marital status. And when we worship love, romance, sex, or marriage—and not God—we welcome the pain and disappointment.

If we are married in this life, it will only be for a brief moment, and we won't regret that brevity ten thousand years from now. We really won't. No one will say, "I really wish I were married," much less, "I really wish I had been married for five or ten more years." Those years will seem like seconds compared with all the gloriously, thoroughly happy time we will have after every marriage ends. We need to think about that as we weigh the intensity of our desperation to have it now. We need to ask if we have made marriage a qualification for a happy and meaningful life. Am I undone and miserable by the prospect of never being married? Do I think of myself as incomplete or insignificant as an unmarried believer? These questions might reveal red flags that warn us marriage has become an idol. Ultimately, we will all be single forever, and it will be gloriously good. Marriage truly is a small and short thing compared with all we have in Christ forever. And I'm writing that as someone who spent more than a decade longing for the temporary this-life experience.

The God of the Universe Is with You

The Bible makes clear that our life is never defined by our performance or circumstances and certainly not by our marital status. What really makes any life worth living today is the presence, protection, and pleasure of the almighty, all-satisfying God. After being sold into slavery by his own brothers, Joseph surprisingly rose to power in perhaps the most dominant empire in the world:

> *The LORD was with Joseph.* . . . His master saw that the LORD was with him and that the LORD caused all that he did to succeed in his hands. So Joseph found favor in his sight and attended him, and he made him overseer of his house and put him in charge of all that he had. (Gen. 39:2–4)

Potiphar put Joseph in charge of everything. But Potiphar's wife lusted after Joseph and tried to seduce him. When he refused her advances, she framed him, claiming he had come on to her. Her lies ripped him from all his power and responsibility and landed him in prison (Gen. 39:20). He committed no sin (at least not with Potiphar's wife); neither was deceit found in his mouth, and yet he was treated as worse than a slave, locked away without any hope of release.

"*But the LORD was with Joseph* and showed him steadfast love and gave him favor in the sight of the keeper of the prison. And the keeper of the prison put Joseph in charge of all the prisoners who were in the prison" (Gen. 39:21–22). Whether in power or in prison, Joseph's life was hope-filled, meaningful, and success-ful, not because he worked so hard or received what he deserved or lived out his big dreams, but because *God was with him.* The Lord was with him in success, the Lord was with him in prison, and the Lord was with him when he rose to power again, over all of Egypt (Gen. 41:39–40).

Love the Life You Never Wanted

Is the life you're currently living the one you always wanted for yourself? Did you think you'd be married by now? What about your job—not what you hoped for? Do you feel like your gifts are being wasted? Do you dream about doing something different with your life? Maybe you wish you were living somewhere else. You long to be closer to home (or farther away).

The reality is that all of us can imagine something better for ourselves than our circumstances today. The *greater* reality is that if you love and follow Jesus, God always writes a better story for you than you would write for yourself. The "better" is based on this: God himself is the best, most satisfying thing you could ever have or experience, and, therefore, fullness of life is ultimately found not in any earthly success, relationship, or accomplishment but in your proximity to God through faith.

The dark side of this good news is that you may have to walk through pain, disappointment, rejection, and suffering for seven or eight (or seventy or eighty) years. The brighter (and prevailing) side says God never makes a mistake in choosing good for you. Everything you experience—expected or unexpected, wanted or unwanted, pleasing or painful—is God's good plan to make you his own (John 10:27–29), to give you himself forever (Ps. 16:11), and to use your life to reveal himself and his glory to the world around you (Isa. 43:25; 1 Cor. 10:31).

A couple thousand years after Joseph, Paul lived and wrote the same things about life:

> I have learned in whatever situation I am to be content. I know how to be brought low, and I know how to abound. In any and every circumstance, I have learned the secret of facing plenty and hunger, abundance and need. I can do all things through him who strengthens me. (Phil. 4:11–13)

What is the secret of joy and contentment in the face of whatever pain and disappointment life brings? It's centering and anchoring our joy and contentment *in Christ* rather than in marriage or anything else in this life. God means for all of us after the wrongly convicted Joseph, the brutally beaten Paul, and his rejected and crucified Son to have their same faith, hope, and joy, even through our pain and suffering. Make him your greatest treasure and ambition and see everything else that happens to you in the light of that infinite pleasure and security. Learn to love the life you have with God, even if it is the life you never wanted.

5

Knowing Everyone but Never Known

In one sense, growing up—from walking as infants, to counting in elementary school, to going out with friends in middle school, to driving in high school, to working in college, to moving out on our own—is all one long journey to independence. Our parents love and support that journey because they want us to be able to survive and succeed in life. They love us like crazy, they want the best for us, and they would do anything for us, but they don't necessarily want to pay for eight years of undergrad or have us still living in their basement when we're forty-four.

We love independence too. In part, we love growing up and becoming independent because we were made to work, to contribute something to the world—"to work it and keep it" (Gen. 2:15). But we also love independence because it brings freedom. We obeyed Mom and Dad while they were bringing home the bacon, but now we're the boss. And we like being the boss. We like choosing how late to stay out and how late to wake up. We like eating what we want when we want. We love doing things on our schedule, when we feel like it. Independence can be depressing at times because it can feel disconnected and lonely, but independence can also be exhilarating because we start to realize what we're capable of and develop our own sense of autonomy.

The not-yet-married life, by nature, cultivates independence. As we move out of the home and out from under our parents' authority, we take on more responsibility. We also typically become less accountable to others. We're on our own now. The longer we're not yet married, the more easily and aggressively we can move into isolation. Independence from our parents becomes independence from everyone. *I* know what I need. *I* pay my bills. *I* decide my schedule. *I* cook my food (or at least pick it up in the drive-through). I'm an adult. I don't need anyone anymore. Independence can breed isolation, and isolation separates us from the grace we need and sets us against the first and greatest calling on our lives. No one was made to be truly single—to live for God's glory solo. Proverbs warns us, "Whoever isolates himself seeks his own desire; he breaks out against all sound judgment" (Prov. 18:1). No one was made to go it alone. Independence is one vital aspect of Christian growth and maturity, but so is dependence— dependence on God and dependence on others around us. Jesus says, "By *this* all people will know that you are my disciples, if you have love for one another" (John 13:35).

Independence Days

Today, we don't think of ourselves as isolated, or at least we wouldn't describe ourselves that way. Everyone has hundreds of Instagram followers or friends on Snapchat. The likes, comments, and attention create this illusion of community. Lots of people know lots of things *about* us. But most of them don't really know us. They see the random moments we decide to share, like a few dozen pieces of a thousand-piece puzzle. No one can see the whole picture on social media. Our streams make us *feel* known without ever allowing us to truly *be* known.

Hebrews says, "Take care, brothers, lest there be in any of you an evil, unbelieving heart, leading you to fall away from the living God. But exhort one another every day, as long as it is called 'today,' that none of you may be hardened by the deceitfulness of sin" (Heb. 3:12–13). Isolated Christians are dead Christians before long. Because of how sin attacks us—living inside of us, lying to our hearts, convincing us that what's false is true—we need others to *regularly* ("every day") remind us what's true and to warn us not to play with sin or indulge in it. Christians are not to be less connected and less dependent as we grow and mature. We are to become *more* connected, *more* dependent, as we wait for Jesus to come back. We exhort one another day after day: turn from sin, run to God, and save your soul. Without those voices, we're doomed. Satan is too compelling, too persuasive, too savvy. He knows us better than we even know ourselves, and he will deceive us to death if we let him.

God can use us to encourage and challenge one another in all kinds of ways, including text messages, tweets, and Snapchat stories, but the massive fight we're fighting is most effectively fought face-to-face and life on life, because we will always be prone to project a different picture of ourselves, a version of ourselves that we like, instead of the real us. The temptation is still there in face-to-face friendships too, but it's so much easier to hide online. Consistently putting ourselves together in the same room immediately makes us more vulnerable.

The author of Hebrews writes, "And let us consider how to stir up one another to love and good works, *not neglecting to meet together*, as is the habit of some, but encouraging one another, and all the more as you see the Day drawing near" (Heb. 10:24–25). The natural drift of our lives will be away from community. Real, substantive, life-changing relationships do not happen or last by accident. It takes effort and intentionality. There will always be a temptation *not* to meet, not to consistently expose ourselves—our decisions, our emotions, our burdens, our sin—to other believers.

I know that, as someone who rode along, year after year, as the third, and fifth, and sometimes even the seventh wheel. The Devil does not want us to be known by brothers and sisters in Christ, because being truly known will bring the kinds of comfort, conviction, healing, and holiness he hates.

A Secret Garden of Pride

One key to walking through pain and disappointment is the people you keep close to you. Suffering may be Satan's favorite way to isolate us. Pain can become a secret garden of pride. We don't talk about it often, because it's so sensitive, so vulnerable—so painful. As touchy as the topic of pain is though, it's equally dangerous to tiptoe around it. At its worst, it can cause us to doubt God's goodness, to wallow in self-pity, and to isolate ourselves from him and from others. Pain becomes proud because it believes no one else understands. *No one feels what I feel.* And so pain distances itself from anyone who might try to speak into its suffering. But God has given us himself, his Word, *and each other* to bring faith, comfort, and strength in the midst of our pain, even the most severe and unique pain.

One test to determine whether our pain is producing pride is to ask how we respond to encouragement from others, maybe especially from other believers who *don't* understand our sadness, loneliness, disappointment, or whatever else we are feeling. Are we willing to hear the hope of God from someone who has not experienced or cannot comprehend our current heartache? If we're unwilling, then our pain has driven us into isolation, and Satan's succeeding in his plans for our suffering.

Case Study: The Pain of Unwanted Singleness

Several years ago I wrote a handful of articles related to singleness while I was still not yet married, and they seemed to be received well. I assume they were liked and shared by many, at least in part because I was a single guy myself reflecting on the hardships (and goodness) in singleness. After I finally married my bride, I was amazed by how quickly I seemed to have lost all credibility with some of the not yet married. Now-barely-married me published an article entitled "Hope for the Unhappily Single." While many expressed appreciation for the article, a new chorus of voices sang out against my writing:

> This is not meant to be disrespectful, but it's hard to take seriously an article on singleness from someone who is married.

> This is just offensive. Only people already married write stuff like this.

> It's always the married people that give you the advice about being satisfied with Jesus. That's real easy for them to say.

The irony is that I wrote the article more than a year before I got married. Afterward, I was saying the same truths, with the same voice, from the same experience, but the words were met with new resistance, even rejection.

The negative comments were not the dominant response, so I'm not telling the story to vindicate the piece or my point of view. In fact, I thought and said some of the same negative things about the "encouragement" I received from married friends. The revelation for me, though, was how easily we all are prone to wield our pain to reject God's good news for us. I see it in myself. We will reject whatever someone says about our pain, even when it's simply repeating *God's* words to us, simply because we don't believe that that person—author, pastor, parent, friend—can relate to what we're going through. Satan loves to see pain and suffering separate us from the body of Christ, growing up like a great wall and cutting us off from the love and encouragement of other Christians.

The First and Greatest Step

Your first step in finding the community you need should be to join a local church. This is one of the most radically countercultural and spiritually beneficial things you can do in the not-yet-married life. When everyone else your age refuses to be tied down and resists being accountable, submit yourself to a body of believers. Drive a stake into the ground and say to the whole world that you belong to Jesus, that your life is his, and that you're willing to have others hold you to that. Tell them Christianity is not a tiny corner of your life; it *is* your life.

You might think that's happening with your friends, but those relationships, as strong and safe as they may seem, are really only held together by affection, not covenant. Something could go south tomorrow and your "community" suddenly vanishes. It's the difference between a dating relationship and a marriage. The covenant establishes the expectations and keeps everyone at the table. Christian friendship is a critical part of the healthy Christian life, but it cannot replace membership in a local church. Even if your friends know you better than anyone at church (and they probably do), they are not qualified or committed (formally) to caring for you when your life starts to fall apart or when you wander into sin. They can walk away like a bored boyfriend. The church is more stable, more safe, and more reliable.

The church should play several important roles in our lives. The weekly gathering will be a much-needed source of refuge and refreshment, where we are washed again with good news and receive God's true and life-giving Word. Becoming a member also ties our specific gifts into a specific body of needy people. We will have more opportunities than ever to be an active and productive part of the body of Christ, sharing what God has given us—to be on mission in our singleness for the sake of others. The church should also be instrumental in helping us discern what to do with our lives. Calling may *begin* in our heart, as God gives us the desire to take that job or marry that girl, but we should never assume God's blessing without confirmation from other believers. Our hearts are too prone to wander, and we're too prone to justify what we want. If life's just about doing what we want to do, then by all means we should isolate ourselves. But if it's about doing what we were made to do, what we have uniquely been gifted and called to do—what will make the most of Jesus—then we have to surround ourselves with people chasing those same things with us. We need to be a member of a church.

To be sure, the church can still fail you. That's why it's important to find a healthy church. Do you get the impression that the people in this church really, genuinely, passionately love Jesus Christ? When you listen to them pray and sing and speak, do they keep coming back to the cross? When the pastor preaches, do you see what he's saying in the Bible, or is most of what he says simply his own thoughts? Are there small groups in this church, or some other place where you can really be known? Do the leaders seem concerned with caring for each member and making sure, to the best of their ability, that you do not fall away in love with sin? There are a lot more questions to ask, but those are some of the most basic and important. We must be a member of a local church, and we should make sure it is a church we can trust with our souls and lives.

Hang Out with Married People

Once you're a part of a local church, be intentional about spending time with and learning from people in other stages of life. It's one of the greatest blessings of being a part of a healthy church, the opportunity to interact with believers who have already experienced what we're experiencing now or are going to experience.

Hang out with married people. The longer you're not yet married, the more time you have to learn about marriage from other people's successes and failures. While you can't avoid your own set of marital missteps and sins, you certainly can increase the odds of successes, small and large, by being a good student beforehand. Look for opportunities to be a regular part of a married person's life and family. If you're not around enough to see any ugliness or messiness, you might not be around enough. Don't impose on people, but don't be afraid to initiate the conversation either. Offer to babysit on date night or help with yard work or bring a meal when one of the kids goes down sick. Then be a student. Ask questions. Take notes on what to imitate. As our minds and hearts are being shaped by Scripture for marriage, we need examples of flawed but faithful marriages. One pastor and his wife had me over for lunch with their family most Sundays for three whole years. I learned a lot more watching him lead and serve at home than from watching him on stage at church.

While married people provide an important perspective and example, you also need people in your life who are experiencing the same feelings, longings, and temptations you are. You should find and invest in people who are asking the same questions as you and also seeking to make the most of this unique season of singleness for Jesus's sake. Think about it: though he was single, Paul did most of his ministry with someone. Find the trusted, gifted, and mission-minded friends in your life and be accountable to one another to make your not-yet-married life matter for the kingdom. Following Christ was never meant to be done alone, even when you're not yet married.

Not-Yet-Married Community

If we are in Christ, there's ultimately nothing single about us. We all know there are intimacies that are—and should be—unique to marriage, but those that matter most really can be experienced in the bride of Christ, his church. A husband or wife may help and provide for us in ways others can't, but a true, Spirit-filled, persistent, and present brother or sister can care for us in remarkable ways.

These relationships, born and built in the gospel, offer us all kinds of love and intimacy. In this love—one for another in the household of faith—we find affection (Rom. 12:10), comfort (2 Cor. 13:11), kindness (Eph. 4:32), relief (Gal. 6:2), encouragement (Eph. 5:19), honesty and truth (Col. 3:9), forgiveness (Col. 3:13), guidance and correction (Col. 3:16), protection (Heb. 3:13), prayer (James 5:16), and hospitality (1 Pet. 4:9). In waiting for our wedding day, we really don't have to wait for any of these things. God has already provided them for us through one another. If we are part of *this* family, we are *not* single. We might not be married, but we are planted in an everlasting community and therefore surrounded with lasting love, affection, security, and a thousand other relational benefits.

These kinds of relationships don't happen by accident. We won't experience the comforts of Christian friendship without working for them. Before anyone can serve us, we need to put ourselves in the path of his or her love. Join a small group, or start one. Find a couple of men (for men) or women (for women) to share life and pray with regularly, even weekly. Serve with a ministry through your church or in the local community, and be intentional about getting to know the people working alongside you. Don't expect helpful, meaningful relationships to just happen to you. It will require a lot of initiative, but we can't live in the fullness of the joy, love, and purpose God promises without this kind of community, *especially* when we're not yet married.

6

100,000 Hours

What should I do with my life? For many not-yet-married people, that question probably translates: *Where should I work?* It's a difficult question and, for many, a constant and ever-changing question, sometimes for years and years. Degrees don't guarantee jobs, and they rarely help us make the big decisions. What city should I live in? What jobs should I apply for? How will I know to accept an offer or to stay in the job I have?

Everyone has to work to live (even if we don't work for a paycheck), and we'll probably spend more time working each week than anything else we do. How do we make the most of that time and tie all of that energy and effort into the things that really matter most to us? As followers of Jesus rescued by Jesus to spend eternity with Jesus, we do not work to prove ourselves or to serve ourselves. But what should we actually *do*? What should *I* do? The practical question is, What will I do for a living? When you do the math—50 hours x 50 weeks x 40 years—and realize we're talking about *100,000* hours, the question really is, What will I *be*?

In our small group alone, over the past several years we've had an engineer, a nurse, an insurance underwriter, a doula, a human resources specialist, a stay-at-home mom, a physical therapist, an in-home caregiver, an accountant, an admissions counselor, a nanny, a soccer coach, an IT consultant, and more. Every one of those jobs carries the potential to be work done for God and his glory. Paul writes, "Whatever you do, work heartily, as for the Lord and not for men, knowing that from the Lord you will receive the inheritance as your reward. You are serving the Lord Christ" (Col. 3:23–24). If we are Christ's, we *are* serving Jesus when we program software, coach high school soccer, sell insurance, care for our home and raise three kids, or manage our massive company's finances. It's not an accident that you work where you work and that you spend most of your time there each week. It's a strategic move by the God of the universe to accomplish his one overarching goal for your life: that the world would know that he is God, that you are his, and that life and joy are only found in him. Elijah said, "O Lord, God of Abraham, Isaac, and Israel, let it be known this day that you are God in Israel, and that I am your servant, and that I have done all these things at your word" (1 Kings 18:36). That should be the banner over all our work, wherever we work, every day that we work.

Work Can Work against Us

Our work has the potential to be a playground for our greatest purpose in life, giving us opportunities on opportunities to use our time and gifts to say that God, not work, money, or success, is our Savior and treasure. But as with every other good gift God gives, work also has the potential to distract us from what matters most, to remove God from the throne of our hearts, and to keep us on the sidelines of the most important work in the world. Why is that an especially relevant warning for the not yet married? Well, because some of us who *want* to be married just put the time, energy, and affection we would be putting into marriage into our career instead. When God doesn't bring the man or woman, we just marry a job. Profession can become the premarital affair of the not yet married—and more so today than ever. When God goes to great lengths to exalt and sanctify marriage, we often downplay it in order to pursue our vocational dreams.

Whatever work we do will be a temptation to trust in ourselves and not in God—to rejoice in and worship what we can see and take credit for instead of the God behind and beneath it all. Yes, Paul said it is better not to be married, but I don't think he had career advancement in mind. We need a calling and a treasure bigger than ourselves and more glorious than any of our work. If we want to be truly happy in our jobs, we cannot base our happiness on our jobs or our abilities. Our worship and happiness must be anchored and rooted first and only in God. He alone has done all the work worthy of worship. With our hands on the plow and our hearts with God, then Peter may say of us, "Though you have not seen him, you love him. Though you do not now see him, you believe in him and rejoice [and work] with joy that is inexpressible and filled with glory" (1 Pet. 1:8).

We Cannot Earn Love

We all try to earn love. For many of us, it started in preschool trying to please Mom and Dad with another picture for the fridge. Then it was cultivated in the competition of middle-school classrooms, and confirmed in the grades and awards of high school. In college, for the first time, we were identified by our major—our future job. And then four years later, after our first paycheck, we're already fighting society's desire to define us by where we work, who works for us, and how much we make. It all *looks* like work, but it's really worship. It wears the name tag of responsibility and provision, but it's often the frantic, promiscuous search for affirmation and redemption.

God will never be won through work. He loves to save, but he will not rescue those who believe they've earned it. Grace is the only currency he trades in. Everything else we might offer him is as Monopoly money in his hands. He refuses to love and affirm you like some cosmic CEO, because he's not "served by human hands, as though he needed anything" (Acts 17:25). To be clear, success is *not* a curse. It becomes a curse when it quietly becomes our savior. God prospers the work of our hands in all kinds of ways for his glory. But it is *not* his method of making us his, and it's certainly not meant to make much of us. We work and succeed as those who've already been rescued from our brokenness and need. Married or not yet married, we labor from the safety of God's love. We won't earn anything from God between 9:00 and 5:00, so we work with the security and confidence we already have *in Christ* because of his cross.

Eight Aims for Every Job

The gospel frees us from going to work to *prove* ourselves, and it frees us from going to work to *serve* ourselves. Maybe we're not aiming at six- or seven-digit salaries, or a newer and nicer car, or recognition and praise from industry leaders, but is our desire for that job driven by a heart for the world around us or for the one within us? Is our work about making our life count for the good of others or about having our own little heaven here? The gospel saves us so deeply *and* satisfies us so fully that we can let ourselves—our gifts, our career, even our lives—be poured out for the sake of others, especially for the sake of their faith and joy in God. Wherever we work, we've been deployed by God as agents of everlasting joy. Here are eight aims that should drive every Christian career path. Fall in love with these aspirations, and your work will bear much fruit for Christ, regardless of your field.

1. *Aspire to make God look great.*

As we've learned already, God's passion for his glory inspires everything he does, including loving and saving sinners (Isa. 44:22–23).

And now he calls the redeemed to do all *we* do for his glory: "Whether you eat or drink, or whatever you do, do all to the glory of God" (1 Cor. 10:31). *Whatever* we do: privately and publicly, recreationally and vocationally, Sunday *and* Monday, single and married. God's greatest work in the world is to reveal a little more of his stunning strength and beauty in the eyes of people everywhere. He wants that to be the heartbeat and aim of our life and vocation as well, wherever we work—that people would see our good work and give our God glory (Matt. 5:16).

2. Aspire to do God's work.

If our only category for the Lord's work is Christian ministry, it won't take us long to functionally disconnect our life's vocation from our life's mission—to make much of God and his glory. *All* work is God's work—prepared by him, carried out by faith in him, and done before him and for him. The accountant's bookkeeping, the developer's programming, and the mother's lunch making are works from God, planned by him long before our first day on the job. All our good works, on and off the clock, were prepared for us in order that we would walk in them (Eph. 2:10).

Our work is God's work because we cannot do it without him. Nothing, vocationally or otherwise, will please God if it is not done in faith, that is, actively trusting in and treasuring Jesus. Paul says, "Whatever does not proceed from faith is sin" (Rom. 14:23). The bus driver's route, the surgeon's precision, and the concierge's counsel are all the Lord's work when they are done in reliance upon him for strength, wisdom, and giftedness. Paul's words, "Whatever you do, work heartily, as for the Lord and not for men. . . . You are serving the Lord Christ," are not a piece of hyperspiritual advice for overcoming psychological barriers in your job. When we love Jesus, in all our work of any kind, we are serving *him*.

3. Aspire to find your joy in God, not money.

"Whom have I in heaven but you? And there is nothing on earth that I desire besides you" (Ps. 73:25). Perhaps no distraction will be more subtly compelling than our career (or the success, fame, and money it brings). With 100,000 hours, our job will have an awful lot of our attention anyway. No one, however, can love God *and* money—or success, recognition, perfectionism, or promotions. It's not that it's bad advice for our health. It's impossible (Matt. 6:24).

We defeat these threats to our soul by keeping ourselves more satisfied in God. Isaiah writes, "Why do you spend your money for that which is not bread, and your labor for that which does not satisfy? Listen diligently to me, and eat what is good, and delight yourselves in rich food" (Isa. 55:2). Someone who eats like this—who feeds himself on all that God is for him forever—will not squander his or her life striving for nicer things or higher steps on the corporate ladder. Maybe God will give us this or that in our work, but it will mean nothing compared to having him (John 4:34). And loving God like that will lead us to all kinds of good decisions about where to work and what to do with the pennies and influence we earn along the way.

4. Aspire to confound the world.

I appeal to you, future employees and employers, "present your bodies as a living sacrifice, holy and acceptable to God, which is your spiritual worship" (Rom. 12:1). Our life—our whole life, including our work—is an act of worship. How? "Do not be conformed to this world, but be transformed by the renewal of your mind" (Rom. 12:2). Will we work in a way that conforms to this world or in a way that confounds it? Spirit-filled followers of Jesus are to be distinctly, noticeably different from people who do not know and love our Lord. When we change the central reality of our life, other things ought to change too.

We want the world to be confused enough about the way we live, work, and spend that they ask about our hope in Christ (1 Pet. 3:15).

5. Aspire to provide for yourself and your family.

This comes naturally to most. We all need to eat, and so we all need to work. Even within the safety and generosity of the church, Paul says, "if anyone is not willing to work, let him not eat" (2 Thess. 3:10). God has made a world in which we survive by contributing to society in tangible, tradable ways. We live by faith, and we eat by work. Most of the world takes this for granted, but God-loving, money-fearing people might overlook it. We serve a providing God (Luke 11:10–13; James 1:17), and we image his providing love for us when we provide for those entrusted to us. Practices like planning, budgeting, and saving are not faithless acts. In fact, that kind of stewardship will glorify God greatly when they're done in love for him and for our (future) families.

It's important to say that this will not always, or even mainly, be financial. Fathers and mothers must provide for each other and their children in a thousand unpaid ways. Providing spiritually and emotionally might even mean setting aside an income or promotion, at least for a season. The principle is to provide for our own, to the best of our ability, in a way that points them (and others) to God's provision for us in Jesus.

6. Aspire to overflow to others.

For the glory of God, we should aspire to provide for ourselves, but it shouldn't end there. God has much more in mind for our money than simply *our* own food, rent, and gasoline. "Let the thief no longer steal, but rather let him labor, doing honest work with his own hands, *so that he may have something to share* with anyone in need" (Eph. 4:28). Paul didn't say, "so that he need not steal from others." No, godly work isn't merely concerned with me. Truly Christian careers, in whatever industry, meet the needs of others. The not yet married can often be even more generous, because we're paying only one person's bills for now. The promise we have from Jesus is, "It is more blessed to give than to receive" (Acts 20:35). We stupidly seek after blessing when we seek it by earning and hoarding. Jesus *promises* we'll be better off—really better off—when we stop keeping for ourselves and liberally let go of what is ours for others. So we should pray (and interview, negotiate, and sign contracts) with this goal in mind—regularly and radically sharing what we have and earn with others (1 Tim. 6:18).

7. Aspire to build and protect the church.

God saves the world through the church (Eph. 3:10). It's his only means of carrying the message of the gospel to all the workplaces and peoples around the world. There isn't a plan B, some undiscovered strategy that might replace the church someday. And our victory through the church is sure (Matt. 16:18), so no true investment there will ever be made in vain. All of our work should be contributing to that great cause. The church is a body made up of lots of members that depend on each other, like eyes and hands and legs (1 Cor. 12:12–26). If we are following Jesus, we *are* part of that body. The question is whether we'll be an active, healthy part. If we're not, the church will suffer. It will lack the unique gifts God has given us to serve her. It could be teaching or counseling or finances or greeting or cooking or driving or a thousand other things. We should have in mind how our 100,000 work hours might serve the local church most.

Amazingly, the greatest work of the church is not ultimately to be done by pastors (those called to vocational ministry) but by laypeople. The shepherds are there "to equip *the saints* for the work of ministry, for building up the body of Christ" (Eph. 4:12).

Pastors equip you and me to do the ministry. That suggests we are just as likely, maybe even more likely, to be engaged in the mission of the church if we're not paid by the church. That makes every nonvocational lover of Jesus incredibly strategic for the kingdom.

8. Aspire to work for what lasts.

Have in mind that this life is short, and everything not done for Christ will be in vain. Defy the deceitful notion that we have to build up and acquire here. Jesus says, "Do not lay up for yourselves treasures on earth, where moth and rust destroy and where thieves break in and steal, but lay up for yourselves treasures in heaven, where neither moth nor rust destroys and where thieves do not break in and steal" (Matt. 6:19–20). This does not necessarily mean doing something explicitly Christian. It does mean that things done for selfish and sinful reasons will not last. We want the investments we make with our time, money, creativity, and talents—with our not-yet-married life and work—to be investments that last into eternity, and they *will* when they tell the world something about our God.

100,000 Opportunities

If those eight aims are our aims, there are 100,000 (and more) good ways for us to spend our 100,000 hours, and the vast majority of them will not pay us to proclaim Christ. Vocational Christian ministry is not the *only* option. In fact, for most of us, the ministry that will make the most of Jesus likely will not be "ministry." Maybe your 100,000 hours will supply the needs of strategic ministries or equip you to serve the church in unique ways (technical, communications, maintenance, and more), or surround you with not-yet-believing people with whom you can more naturally share the gospel. Be open to a specific call of God on your life to vocational ministry, but don't think that is the only option for effective, faithful, and fruitful ministry. Whether we're writing sermons at a desk, selling desks, putting them together, harvesting the lumber, or raising the lumberjack's kids to be godly men and women, God can use the not yet married uniquely and powerfully for his one great cause in the world.

7

Procrastination in Pursuing Him

Singleness is a horrible and popular excuse for persisting in sin. In our pursuit of marriage, we often permit ourselves to fall into holding patterns in our growth and maturity. We're so focused on finding love that we get distracted from killing sin. But we are always being either conformed to the world around us or transformed into something entirely new and different (Rom. 12:1–2). There's no lazy middle ground for us to rest on for a few years while we wait for a wife or husband. Singleness can become a roundabout in our walk with Jesus. We set out after Christ, make a lot of changes early on, and then suddenly find ourselves driving in circles. The car's still moving, but we're not making progress, and we hit some of the same potholes over and over again. Sometimes we get so distracted—so entertained and contented in the world—that we forget where we were even going in the first place.

Perhaps the greatest loss in the not-yet-married life is growth in godliness, because so many of us procrastinate in pursuing it, waiting until we get married to get more serious. We don't have the day-in, day-out accountability of a spouse and family yet—

people close enough to see how we really live. And we foolishly think finding love will mysteriously unlock growth and maturity in our lives. It's true that marriage often brings sanctification, but the testimony of most is that marriage is more diagnosis than prescription in our pursuit of godliness. Rather than unlocking the fruit of the Spirit, it will more often (graciously) uncover flaws. In reality, none of the fruits of the Spirit are reserved for marriage. They're the produce of conversion (our union with Christ), not of marriage (our union with a spouse). Fortunately for the not yet married, the union that matters most doesn't require a license from our local county administrator.

Paul says the key to experiencing the freedom purchased for us at the cross is to walk increasingly like Jesus—to skip the roundabouts and ride on the highway of the gospel—putting on our new self by the power of the Spirit (Gal. 5:16). We turn away from the desires of the flesh and trade them for better ones—love, joy, peace, patience, kindness, goodness, faithfulness, gentleness, and self-control (Gal. 5:22–23). The free and full life is found in Christ and played out in Christlikeness.

Nine Lies in the Not-Yet-Married Life

But we have an enemy in this search—an anti-gardener. Satan is the father of lies (John 8:44), and the spoiler of spiritual produce. His lies are his most effective means of distracting us and starving us of this soul-satisfying fruit. They're the murderously misplaced signs keeping us driving round and round. Lies about you. Lies about your past. Lies about marriage. Lies about your future spouse. Lies about your friends and family. And if we're not careful as single people, we might find ourselves with a lot more time alone to listen to them. Following are nine deceptions that the not yet married need to defeat, each with a weapon from God's Word—a road map for avoiding roundabouts.

*Lie 1: I'm selfish only because I'm still single, and I
don't have anyone to care for my needs and feelings.*

Sure, selfishness might be just as rampant in marriage, and certainly more visible, but the single life by nature caters to and cultivates it. Each day you make most of your decisions based on what you need and want, and no one really knows the difference. But as promising as self-centeredness and self-gratification might seem in the moment, *love* offers us a better promise. "Beloved, let us love one another, for love is from God, and whoever loves has been born of God and knows God" (1 John 4:7). This God and this love are available to the married and not yet married alike.

*Lie 2: I'm anxious only because I'm still single, and I
don't know if God will ever bring me a spouse.*

There may be more *intense* anxieties among young people in our churches than their unfulfilled desires for marriage, but there may not be a more prevalent one. Fears and grief over love, relationships, and marriage steal a lot of sleep and energy from not-yet-married people. Preoccupation with and self-pity in our inadequacies promise to make us feel better, but they lack any real power to help. But God can give us real *peace*: "Do not be anxious about anything, but in everything by prayer and supplication with thanksgiving let your requests be made known to God. And the peace of God, which surpasses all understanding, will guard your hearts and your minds in Christ Jesus" (Phil. 4:6–7). Whether you meet your future spouse this afternoon or live alone the rest of your life, God really can give you peace-filled rest and perspective at every point along the way, if you'll ask him for it.

*Lie 3: I'm impatient only because I'm still single,
and I've waited a long time to be married.*

Amazon, Netflix, and smartphones have depreciated *patience*. Instant gratification has gratified us enough to make us forget how priceless and beautiful patience really is. God promises through Paul, "To those who by patience in well-doing seek for glory and honor and immortality, he will give eternal life" (Rom. 2:7). There are some things we can have only through patience. Glory. Honor. Immortality. God. No technology will ever speed up the process. And the muscles we need to wait well for God are built in our waiting for lesser things, such as weddings. All our waiting is worth it, if *through* it we get more of the one for whom our souls are all ultimately waiting.

Lie 4: I don't need to worry about other people's needs and problems right now, because I'm still single, and I have a hard enough time dealing with my own stuff.

Entitlement is one of the great dangers of singleness. It creeps into everything, but at its core it convinces us to focus exclusively on ourselves—a kind of survival mentality—often at the expense of others. As entitlement and self-preoccupation grow and invade our hearts, we become less interested in and compassionate toward others. But the life-giving fruit of the Spirit is *kindness*—an attitude of friendly sympathy and generosity. "Be *kind* to one another, tenderhearted, forgiving one another, as God in Christ forgave you" (Eph. 4:32). The beautiful, liberating promise behind our kindness is the kindness of God to us in Christ. Those who put on Christ—and are found to be kind in him—have received kindness from an almighty, holy God despite what they deserve.

Lie 5: I'm not as far along in holiness because I don't have anyone around to challenge me. I'll focus on those things when I get married and have a family.

One excuse for procrastination in our pursuit of holiness is that not-yet-married Christians are not yet accountable in the same ways as married Christians, as if we're somehow less human. When we have wives or husbands or children who are affected by

our attitudes and behaviors, then it will really matter who we are
and how we act. When a man and woman get married, they do
become one, but not more *fully* one than any single believer. Each
and every Spirit-filled child of God is accountable to God regardless of his or her marital status (Rom. 14:12). "Blessed are those
who hunger and thirst for righteousness, for they shall be satisfied"
(Matt. 5:6). Blessed—"happy"—are single men and women who
love and pursue *goodness*, virtue, and integrity. And the blessing
comes right now in your not-yet-married, not-yet-perfect pursuit
of God and his righteousness. With God's power at work in you,
supplement your faith and singleness with goodness (2 Pet. 1:3–5).

Lie 6: I'm flaky and unreliable only because I'm
still single, and you can't really expect single
people to make or keep commitments.

At our worst, some of us really love this about singleness. Those
of us who haven't settled down feel the freedom to move from one
thing to the next, to leave old responsibilities and obligations for
fresh, new things. It could be a new job or church or relationship
or even city. Some changes are good and even necessary, but a lot
of changes are evidence of our refusal to commit and stay. Some
put off marriage in order to avoid commitment altogether and
to keep their felt freedom. But as free as flakiness feels, the Bible
teaches us to love *faithfulness*, devotion, and fidelity in every stage
of life. "Therefore, my beloved brothers, be steadfast, immovable,
always abounding in the work of the Lord, knowing that in the
Lord your labor is not in vain" (1 Cor. 15:58). When it seems on
the outside that it might not be worth it anymore, we rest, work,
and *stay*, knowing every sacrifice in this life for the sake of Christ
is never sacrificed in vain. In the Spirit, against all the patterns of
the twentysomethings around us, we can set aside our selfish and
impulsive ambitions and be slow to walk away from God's work,
however hard and uncelebrated it might be.

Lie 7: I'm harsh with others only because I'm still single, and they don't understand how hard I have it.

Our responses to being harmed say a lot about the state of our hearts. How do you react to people who misunderstand, overlook, or minimize the pain of your singleness? Though good-intentioned, they unwittingly offend you with their advice, questions, or indifference. You feel justified in your anger, expressed in an insensitive or sarcastic word, or in a violent, bitter thought toward them. But God rewards *gentleness* in the face of offense.

He encourages us and our leaders to patiently endure evil, "correcting opponents with *gentleness*. God may perhaps grant them repentance leading to a knowledge of the truth" (2 Tim. 2:25). Ultimately, God corrects and directs hearts. We're not called to inflict judgment on one another but to clothe ourselves in the grace and gentleness God has shown us—grace and gentleness that look like Jesus hanging on a cross for our sins. You might be right to be offended, and you should tell the brother or sister how they made you feel, but you will not solve the offense with a second offense. God calls us instead to gentleness and promises to do the harder work of redemption or retaliation on our behalf.

Lie 8: I'm undisciplined and keep sinning only because I'm still single. The freedom feels good and no one knows, cares, or is affected by my behavior.

There's no unchecked life like the not-yet-married life. It can be easy to live wildly and unwisely when we live in isolation. Our flesh wants us to eat more of this, drink more of that, buy more of this, and watch more of that. None of these things is necessarily bad, but our unchecked sinful cravings will eventually lead us into more sin and idolatry. Enjoying all God has created, as God intended, will require *self-control*—saying no enough to show that we enjoy him more than any of his gifts.

"Every athlete exercises self-control in all things. They do it to receive a perishable wreath, but we an imperishable" (1 Cor. 9:25). When we forsake food, drink, television, sports, shopping, websites, or *anything* in this life for the sake of having and enjoying Christ, we take another step toward an infinite, imperishable inheritance kept in heaven for us (Matt. 6:20; 1 Pet. 1:4). Marriage can offer the up-close-and-personal accountability we might not have in our singleness. Self-control, though, is a fruit of the Spirit, not of a spouse. Look to God for strength, "for it is *God* who works in you, both to will and to work for his good pleasure," and for your self-control (Phil. 2:13).

For many of you, especially men, but women too, the sin you keep punting and putting off is sexual lust and pornography.[5] You lack the self-control not to look or click. I know the enticing enslavement of pornography firsthand, having fought and lost, on and off, through high school and college. Pornography devours as much or more square feet of spiritual ground as any other threat to the church today. However harmless or private it may seem, it is not. It lulls us to sleep. But it's not sleep; it's death. It feels like a short, comfortable nap, but we never wake up. And pornography is force-fed to us in our society, pouring out of every pore of our media and technology.

Whole books have been written on our battle against sexual temptation and sin. I have an entire chapter on sexual purity later in this book. One of the light bulb moments for me, though, in my journey to victory was realizing that it wasn't *only* a self-control issue. The fruits of the Spirit don't work or grow like that. Our broken desires for images or videos suggest all the fruits are rotting, not just self-control. Our fight for purity is not merely a fight for self-control. It's also a pursuit and expression of love, peace, patience, kindness, goodness, faithfulness, gentleness, and joy. When we focus on willpower and self-denial and neglect the rest, we rob ourselves of most of the weapons God has given us for the war. Don't just fight for self-control. Fight for *joy*. Those who choose to see less today will see more forever (Matt. 5:8).

Lie 9: I'm depressed and miserable only because I'm still single, and I won't really be happy until I get married.

Any not-yet reality in our lives is accompanied with pain and longing. Unwanted singleness can be very lonely, and loneliness can be miserable. In those moments, the really compelling lie is that marriage will be the most satisfying solution. Sadly, looking to marriage and a spouse to fill the hole only God can fill will only leave us more depressed and hurt. God graciously gives us another answer for *joy* (Ps. 16:11). In Jesus—*the* way, *the* truth, and *the* life—God has shown us the paths of life and happiness, and it's not the path between the pews at our future wedding. It's the scandalous marriage of a holy God to his chosen, sinful, and forgiven bride, the church. Jesus says, "These things I have spoken to you, that my *joy* may be in you, and that your joy may be *full*" (John 15:11).

The seed of every other fruit of the Spirit is a deep, enduring joy and satisfaction in Jesus. A lack of love communicates that we treasure ourselves more than Jesus and the people he purchased by his blood. Our anxiety tells God we're not happily content to have him and his fatherly plan (and timing) for our lives. Impatience says the Jesus we already have is not enough for us. An inability to say no suggests we believe this food, that purchase, or this website will make us more happy than Jesus. But real joy in Jesus, through the gospel, will free us from all the rotting, poisonous fruit of sin and replace it with new and Spirit-filled attitudes and habits.

Weeding God's Garden in You

If we want to grow the fruit of the Spirit—the fullest, ripest, most delicious fruit—we have to weed the garden. Wherever fruit is not growing (and often even where it is), sin creeps in, sprouts up quickly and quietly, and before long takes over, poisoning any existing fruit and preventing any more from developing. My wife and I have two planters in our backyard, probably 3 feet by 4 feet and filled with soil. It appears the previous owners built them to grow plants and herbs. It also appears they did not succeed in that mission. When we bought the house, they were two wooden amusement parks for weeds, the main attraction being some kind of mutant cabbage. We ignored them the first summer, just cutting the grass around the boxes. After a month or two, they stood three or four feet tall, towering over the rest of our otherwise decently manicured lawn.

Some of us have allowed sins to grow off in the corner of our lives. We build little wooden boxes around them to keep them from spreading anymore. We make plans for what we'll do about them next spring, or maybe the year after. We find a thousand other things to keep us busy, and we take great care of the rest of our life, mowing week after week to make sure the yard looks acceptable to guests. But sin won't be boxed or caged in a corner. Any sin we allow to remain in our lives spreads quickly and quietly, like a virus, into every other area of our heart and relationships. With eternity at stake, and Jesus welcoming us with open arms, arms that were nailed to the cross *for* our sin, we cannot afford to wait another year, or month, or week to attack the root of the sins that entangle us. We have to take the planter by storm today, invading and conquering every weed with grace.

Follow all the fruits of the Spirit down to the root of your sin, whatever your besetting sins, and find victory while you're still single. It will prepare you to date well now, and it will serve your future marriage and ministry in ways you cannot even comprehend. Refuse to procrastinate in killing your sin, and run after the one who wants to make you new.

8

The Secret Most Important Step

There might be a million and one ways for you to apply what you've read so far, but the most important step you can take today is to pray. God means for our lives—married or unmarried, student or employee, young or old—to run on the power of prayer. Prayer fuels the engine of our heart and mind. It's not coffee, or Chipotle, or social media buzz; it's prayer. We need God in and through prayer more than we need anything else. We will not do anything of any real and lasting value without God, which means we will not do anything of any real and lasting value without prayer. And yet you probably feel as insecure about your prayer life as you feel about anything. We know we need to pray, but we know we don't pray enough. And we're not always sure we're even doing it right when we do pray. Should I even be asking God for this? Should I *still* be asking God for this? Do I even know what I need?

We often skip prayer because it makes us uncomfortable and because we don't necessarily see immediate results. But the Bible is clear: prayer is not a side dish for followers of Jesus. It's the oven. God meant for every other part of our lives to be prepared and refined through prayer.

- How do we see and understand more of God and his will for us? "We have not ceased *to pray* for you, asking that you may be filled with the knowledge of his will in all spiritual wisdom and understanding" (Col. 1:9). Spiritual wisdom and understanding—greater insight into God and his plan for us—are found on the far side of prayer.

- How do we remind ourselves that God is our greatest treasure, the only one who will ever truly make us happy? We *pray*, "Whom have I in heaven but you? And there is nothing on earth that I desire besides you. My flesh and my heart may fail, but God is the strength of my heart and my portion forever" (Ps. 73:25–26).

- Where do we find hope and strength to carry out the mission Jesus has given us in the world? "*Pray* also for us, that God may open to us a door for the word, to declare the mystery of Christ" (Col. 4:3). We may do the speaking, but God does the real work, running out ahead of us to open doors for the gospel.

- How do we guard ourselves against all the distractions around us? We keep ourselves spiritually awake through prayer. "[*Pray*] *at all times* in the Spirit, with all prayer and supplication. To that end, keep alert with all perseverance, making supplication for all the saints" (Eph. 6:18).

- How do we persevere through our deepest pains and disappointments? "Is anyone among you suffering? Let him *pray*" (James 5:13).

- And how do we live together in community as believers? Those in the early church "devoted themselves to the apostles' teaching and the fellowship, to the breaking of bread *and the prayers*" (Acts 2:42).

- How do we keep ourselves from checking out of our faith and mission when we clock in at work? "Do not be anxious about *anything*, but in *everything by prayer* and supplication with thanksgiving let your requests be made known to God" (Phil. 4:6). Not just at mealtimes, but before our next meeting. Not just during our morning devotions, but during our next shift. Not just in worship on Sunday, but while we wash clothes on Tuesday. Before we go to work, while we work, and after we work, we take anything and everything to God in prayer.

- What hope do we have for overcoming our sin and experiencing real change and growth? "To this end we always *pray* for you, that our God may make you worthy of his calling and may fulfill every resolve for good and every work of faith by his power" (2 Thess. 1:11). We bring the desire, the resolve, and the faith, but God brings the power. We invite him to keep working on us, with all of his infinite power, love, and creativity, through prayer.

Singleness can be a long, lonely, and confusing season, especially when it's unwanted. There were times in my life, through most of my twenties, when I felt as though I had been *born* wanting to be married. Over those years of waiting, wanting, and wondering why not yet, I learned that God does not guarantee any human experience for his children—not physical health, not marriage, not success at work, not children. And that's because he is utterly, relentlessly committed to giving his precious sons and daughters what's best for them, *when* it's best for them, and only *if* it's best for them. Never otherwise (Rom. 8:28). No matter how good the gift seems to be, or how much we want it, or how long we have waited, God will not abandon the greater good he has promised us (2 Cor. 12:7–10).

But we will be tempted to abandon him, to give up on his plan for us. We really do convince ourselves that we know better, that we can choose better for ourselves than God can—the same God who came and died at infinite cost to save us. But we don't, and we can't. When we begin to feel overlooked or forgotten, or to doubt God's love for us, we distance ourselves from him, when we should be running to him. Instead of walking away, we really need to kneel down and pray. If you don't know where to start in prayer—how to begin talking to God daily, or how to surrender your desires and experiences to him—the following are nine prayers for the not yet married, each with God's words to help shape your longing and waiting.

1. Not my will, but yours, be done.

Jesus knelt down and prayed, saying, "Father, if you are willing, remove this cup from me. Nevertheless, not my will, but yours, be done." (Luke 22:41–42)

"Not my will, but yours, be done." Heavenly Father, if those seven words and the faith beneath them were enough to carry Jesus through the cross for my sake, they should be enough to carry me through anything in this life for his sake. Prepare me to make the most of marriage or singleness, whatever you have chosen and planned for me. If it's not your will for me to marry, help me see all that you have planned for me—my gifts, my ministry, my singleness. Either way, anchor my heart firmly in you.

2. Reveal as much of yourself to me as possible while I'm still single.

[May] the God of our Lord Jesus Christ, the Father of glory, give you the Spirit of wisdom and of revelation in the knowledge of him, having the eyes of your hearts enlightened, that you may know what is the hope to which he has called you, what are the riches of his glorious inheritance in the saints, and what is the immeasurable greatness of his power toward us who believe. (Eph. 1:16–19)

Father, show me more of yourself and shape my life to reveal your glory. As I walk back out on the raging sea of life and of singleness, still my faith in you and set my eyes on you, the one standing strong and reliable above it all. Reveal how much bigger and more beautiful you are than marriage, or any other dream or desire I might have.

3. Satisfy me so fully now that I never look to anyone else to make me happy.

Satisfy us in the morning with your steadfast love,
    that we may rejoice and be glad all our days. (Ps. 90:14)

You, Lord, are the only one who could ever truly make me happy. No spouse, no friend, no job, no amount of money could ever fill the hole inside of me made for you. You are more than enough for me, and yet my heart is still prone to wander. Order my loves according to your surpassing worth and beauty, and guard my eyes and mind from being preoccupied with anyone or anything besides you. Capture my heart again, and secure it against all of Satan's lies.

4. Tell the world about yourself through my joy and freedom in singleness.

Let no one despise you for your youth, but set the believers an example in speech, in conduct, in love, in faith, in purity. (1 Tim. 4:12)

Father, use me and my gifts to make your name great in the world. I want my life to count for the mission you have given us. I want it to count today, even while I am still young and single. Fill me with ambition, creativity, and selflessness for the sake of your glory.

5. Give me faith to trust you even when I walk alone through pain and disappointment.

A thorn was given me in the flesh, a messenger of Satan to harass me, to keep me from becoming conceited. Three times I pleaded with the Lord about this, that it should leave me. But he said to me, "My grace is sufficient for you, for my power is made perfect in weakness." Therefore I will boast all the more gladly of my weaknesses, so that the power of Christ may rest upon me. (2 Cor. 12:7–9)

Help me, Lord, to see every loss or disappointment, every moment of loneliness, every unfulfilled dream or desire, and every evidence of weakness as opportunities to remember and enjoy the strength, hope, and rest you bought for me with the blood of your Son. Remind me that you are working all this, every inch, in every way, for my good.

6. Send me the people I need to follow you.

He gave the apostles, the prophets, the evangelists, the shepherds and teachers, to equip the saints for the work of ministry, for building up the body of Christ. . . . Speaking the truth in love, we are to grow up in every way into him who is the head, into Christ, from whom the whole body, joined and held together by every joint with which it is equipped, when each part is working properly, makes the body grow so that it builds itself up in love. (Eph. 4:11–16)

Surround me with people who love me, and who love you, Father, more than they love me, especially while I live alone. Reveal things about me to me through their eyes, their faith and maturity, and their words. Make me a healthier, more effective member of the local church. Give me a deep, abiding, and growing desire to serve her in whatever ways I can. Rescue me from the blindness and self-centeredness of isolation.

7. Protect me from making work my god while I wait for marriage.

Whatever you do, work heartily, as for the Lord and not for men, knowing that from the Lord you will receive the inheritance as your reward. You are serving the Lord Christ. (Col. 3:23–24)

Help me see any success or progress as evidence of your grace, Lord, and wean me off the love of money and human approval. Liberate me from the tyranny of today's to-do list and receive every task, every meeting, every chore, and every project as an act of worship.

8. Keep me from conforming to the world around me and make me more like Jesus.

It is my prayer that your love may abound more and more, with knowledge and all discernment, so that you may approve what is excellent, and so be pure and blameless for the day of Christ, filled with the fruit of righteousness that comes through Jesus Christ, to the glory and praise of God. (Phil. 1:9–11)

Finish the work you have started within me and through me, Father, making me a little more like Jesus every day. Restrain me from doing anything to make his death look cheap or meaningless. Equip me to increasingly think, talk, and act like someone who has been saved at infinite cost and entrusted with the greatest news the world has ever known.

9. If you have called me to marry, help me to date differently.

Do nothing from selfish ambition or conceit, but in humility count others more significant than yourselves. Let each of you look not only to his own interests, but also to the interests of others. Have this mind among yourselves, which is yours in Christ Jesus, who, though he was in the form of God, did not count equality with God a thing to be grasped, but emptied himself, by taking the form of a servant, being born in the likeness of men. And being found in human form, he humbled himself by becoming obedient to the point of death, even death on a cross. (Phil. 2:3–8)

If you would have me marry, Father, prepare me to love a husband or wife with the love and grace you have shown me through Jesus and his cross. Give me clarity in dating, and guard me from all impurity. Let patience, selflessness, and humility mark every relationship—every date, every conversation, every step forward or backward. In every step of my pursuit of marriage, make it clear that you are God and I am yours.

It may feel as though all the most important things happen when other people are around and watching, but Jesus says the most important step happens while we are alone. "When you pray, go into your room and shut the door and pray to your Father who is in secret. And your Father who sees in secret will reward you" (Matt. 6:6). Are you ready to take the step that no one will see? Will you trust God to meet you there and reward you with more of himself? We can't let prayer sit on the edge of our priorities. We have to bathe all our priorities in prayer. Our waiting and longing should be shaped by and filled with prayer. Our search for purpose and direction in singleness should begin with prayer. Our pursuit of joy should be a journey of prayer.

Part 2

WHEN THE NOT YET MARRIED MEET

9

Date for More Than Marriage

Dating is dead. So says the media. Girls, stop expecting guys to make any formal attempt at winning your affections. Don't sit around waiting for a boy to make you a priority, communicate his intentions, or even call you on the phone. Exclusivity and intentionality are ancient rituals, things of the past, and misplaced hopes.

I beg to differ. It's not that this new line of thinking is necessarily untrue today, or that it's not the current and corrupt trend of our culture. It's just wrong. One of our most precious pursuits, that of a lifelong partner, is tragically being relegated to texts, Snaps, and Tinder swipes, to ambiguous flirtation and fooling around. It's wrong.

There is a God. And this God created and rules his world, including men, women, the biological impulses that bind them together, and the institution that declares their union and keeps it sacred and safe. Therefore, only he can prescribe the purpose, parameters, and means of our marriages. If fullness of life could be found in sexual stimulation, or if it was just a matter of making babies, the "forget formality and just have sex" approach might temporarily satisfy cravings and cause enough conception. But God had much more in mind with romance than orgasms or even procreation, and so should we. So must we. When people in the world are expecting less and less of each other in dating, God isn't. So among the not yet married, we have to work harder in our relationships to preserve what marriage ought to picture and provide.

Mom, Where Do Weddings Come From?

I had my first girlfriend in the sixth grade, my first kiss that summer (different girl), and then a new serious girlfriend almost every year through high school. From far too young, I was looking for affection, safety, and intimacy from girls instead of God. I dated earlier than most, and more than most. My teenage years were one long string of relationships that were too serious for our age, went on too long, and, therefore, ended too painfully. I said, "I love you," too soon, and to too many. My singleness quickly became a reminder, through most of my twenties, that I had messed up, missed opportunities, or done it wrong.

Maybe dating has been hard for you too, for these reasons or others. Maybe Mr. (or Mrs.) Right has started to look like Mr. (or Mrs.) Myth. Maybe you've wanted the relationship or liked the guy or girl, and you've never had the chance. Maybe all the suggestions and advice you've collected have become a confusing mess of good-intentioned contradictions and ambiguity. It's enough to leave you like an eight-year-old, asking, "Mom, where do weddings come from?"

The vision of marriage we see in God's Word—the beautiful, radical display of God's infinite, persevering love for sinners—makes it worth it to date, and date well. The world's approach can provide fun and sex and children, and eventually even some level of commitment and stability, but it cannot lead to the life-giving Jesus after whom our marriages are to take their cues. Friends who enjoy sex with "no strings attached" will find pleasure but not the peaks waiting on the other side of mutual promises. The happiness of marriage is not only or even mainly physical. With the sex, there ought to be a deep sense of safety, a sense of being loved and accepted for who you are, a desire to please without the need to impress. When God engineered the sexual bond between a man and a woman, he made something much more satisfying than the act itself.

Those who recklessly give themselves to a love life of dating without really dating, of romantic rendezvous without Christ and commitment, are settling. They're settling for less than God intended and less than he made possible by sending his Son to rescue and repurpose our lives, including our love lives, for something more. More happiness. More security. More purpose. And the more is found in a mutual faith in and following of Jesus. With this "more," we can say to the watching world, don't settle for artificial and thin loyalty, affection, security, and sexual experimentation when God intends and promises so much more through a Christian union.

How Then Shall We Date?

For those whose roads are marked, like my own, more by mistakes than selflessness, patience, and sound judgment, take hope in the God who truly and mysteriously blesses our broken roads and redeems us from them and who can begin in us a new, pure, wise, godly pursuit of marriage today. Following are some principles for our not-yet marriages. It's not a comprehensive or exhaustive list but simply lessons I've learned and hope can be a blessing for you, your boyfriend or girlfriend, and your future spouse.

1. Know what makes a marriage worth having.

In our worst moments, our objectives are small and misguided. We don't want to be alone on a Friday night anymore. We want to post almost candid, artistically framed pictures with someone on a bridge. We want a guilt-free way to enjoy sex. We want a guy or girl to tell us we're handsome and funny and smart and good at our job. If marriage offered us only these things, though, it really wouldn't be worth it. Many will try to deny that, but the divorce statistics are enough to establish that marriage asks more of us than we ever could have imagined on our wedding day. Most of my married friends would say that what seems fun and pretty and unbreakable at the altar did not feel as clean or easy even days into their lives together. It's still intensely good and beautiful, but it's costly, too costly for small aims.

Before we begin dating, we have to develop a vision for what makes marriage worth having. Why do we even want to be married in the first place? We'll answer this more fully in chapter 11, but it's important for each of us to answer it for ourselves before we start to date. Marriage is worth having because you get *God* in your lifelong commitment to one another. Marriage is about knowing God, worshiping God, depending on God, displaying God, and being made like God. God made man and woman *in his image* and joined them together, giving them unique responsibilities to care for one another in their broken but beautiful union. What makes marriage worth having is that you, your spouse, and those around you see more of God and his love in Jesus. If you're not experiencing that with your boyfriend, break up with him.

If that's not our priority, we need to get a new game plan and probably a new scorecard for our next significant other.

2. It really is as simple as they say.

In a day when people are marrying later and later, and when more and more are resorting to online matchmaking, we probably need to be reminded that marriage really is less about compatibility than commitment. After all, there has never been a less compatible relationship than a holy God and his sinful bride, and that's the mold we're aiming for in our marriages. There is a reason the Bible doesn't have a book devoted to how to choose a spouse. It was not an oversight by the God over all of history, as if he couldn't see into the twenty-first century. The qualifications are wonderfully clear and simple: (1) They must believe your God: "Do not be unequally yoked with unbelievers" (2 Cor. 6:14). (2) They must be of the opposite sex: "Therefore a *man* shall leave his father and his mother and hold fast to his *wife*, and they shall become one flesh" (Gen. 2:24, see also Matt. 19:4–6; Eph. 5:24–32).

Now, there is obviously more involved in discernment while dating. Apart from questions of attraction and chemistry, which are not insignificant, the Bible articulates some roles for wives and husbands. A man ought to protect and provide for his wife (Eph. 5:25–29). Women ought to help and submit to their man (Gen. 2:18; Eph. 5:22–24). Fathers ought to lead their families in God's Word (Eph. 6:4). Parents must love and raise their children in the faith (Deut. 6:7). So admittedly we are looking for more than an attractive person of the opposite sex who "loves Jesus."

That said, many of us need to be reminded that God's perfect person for each of us isn't all that perfect. Every person who marries is a sinner. Therefore, the search for a spouse isn't a pursuit of perfection but a mutually flawed pursuit of Jesus. It is a faith-filled attempt to become like him and to make him known with another. Regardless of the believer you marry, you will likely find out soon enough that you do not feel as "compatible" as you once did, but hopefully you will marvel more at God's love for you in Jesus and the amazing privilege it is to live out that love together, especially in light of your differences and inadequacies.

3. Pursue clarity more than intimacy.

The greatest danger of dating is giving parts of our hearts and lives to someone to whom we're not married. It is a significant risk, and many men and women have deep and lasting wounds from relationships because a couple enjoyed emotional or physical closeness without a lasting, durable commitment. Cheap intimacy feels real for the moment, but you get what you pay for.

While the great prize in *marriage* is Christ-centered intimacy, the great prize in *dating* is Christ-centered clarity. Intimacy is safest in the context of marriage, and marriage is safest in the context of clarity. The purpose of our dating is to determine whether the two of us should get married, so we should focus our effort there. In our pursuit of clarity, we will undoubtedly develop intimacy, but we ought not do so too quickly or naïvely. Be intentional and outspoken to one another that, as Christians, intimacy before marriage is dangerous, while clarity is unbelievably precious. We will focus more on pursuing clarity in dating in chapter 12.

4. Wait to date until you can marry.

If all of our dating should be aimed at marriage, why do so many of us date before we can marry?[6] Why did I have a girlfriend when I was twelve (and thirteen, and fourteen, and fifteen, and so on)? At age twelve, I'm sure I really *believed* I might marry my girlfriend, even though I couldn't marry her for eight or even ten more years. Think about that. *If* we had gotten married when we graduated college, it would have taken us *ten years* to be married as long as we had been pursuing marriage. If we're honest, we don't pursue marriage as teenagers. We pursue attention, affection, significance, and security. And as we pursue and prioritize those things over God and marriage (subtly at first, and then more blatantly later on), we welcome the chaos, confusion, heartache, and temptation of dating when we can't marry, when we can't bring dating to its good and intended goal.

Some of us might be born wanting to be married, but none of us are born ready to be married. Legally, we can't marry until we're eighteen, except in Nebraska and Mississippi, where we must be even older (nineteen and twenty-one, respectively). Beyond the law, there are serious questions of our maturity and stability. Has our boyfriend or girlfriend matured enough to have any idea what they might be like as a husband or wife for the next fifty years? Have we? Will one or both of us be able to provide for a family financially? Has his or her faith in Jesus been tested enough by trials to be confident it's real? Some of you will hate this advice—I'm sure I would have—but we all need to acknowledge that we can date long before we can marry. But that doesn't mean we should. It's almost impossible to date toward marriage when marriage isn't even on the radar yet. You may be dreaming about marriage already, but is it realistic that the two of you could marry anytime soon? Before college, probably not. If I could go back and do it all over again (and I wish I could), I would wait to date until I could marry. My advice—take it or leave it—is to wait until you can reasonably marry him or her in the next eighteen months. It doesn't mean you have to marry that quickly. The important part is that you *could*, if God made it clear this was his will and his timing for you.

5. Find a fiancée on the front lines.

Instead of making marriage your mission, make it God's global cause and the advance of the gospel where you are, and look for someone pursuing the same. If you're hoping to marry someone who passionately loves Jesus and makes him known, it's probably best to put yourself in a community of people committed to that. Join a small group, not just a group of single Christians but one actively on mission together. Get plugged into a ministry in your church that's engaging the lost in the local community. Focus on the harvest, and you're bound to find a helper.

This does not mean that we should serve *because* we might find love. God is not ultimately honored with that kind of self-serving service. No, it simply means that if we're looking for a particular kind of person, there are good, safe, identifiable places where those kinds of people live, serve, and worship together. Get involved in a community like that, serve each other, and look for God to open doors for dating.

6. Don't let your mind marry him before the rest of you can.

While this may seem to be much more common among women, I was single long enough and around enough single guys to know it's not exclusively a female problem. The trajectory of all truly Christian romance ought to be marriage, so it should not surprise us that our dreams and expectations—our hearts—race out ahead of everything else. It simply isn't that hard to imagine what our children would look like, or where we would vacation together, or how family holidays would work, or what kind of house we might buy. And just like sex, all these things could be really good, safe, and beautiful, but in the context of a covenant. Satan wants to subtly help us build marriage and family idols that are too fragile for our not-yet-married relationships. "He told me he loved me." "She said she would never leave." They're the seemingly priceless sentences that don't always cash. They're often said with good intentions but without the ring—and without a ring, the results can be devastating. Pace yourself in every aspect of the relationship—emotional, spiritual, physical. Guard your heart and imagination from running out ahead of your current commitment.

7. Boundaries make for the best of friends.

The most oft-asked dating question among Christians might be, "How far is too far before marriage?" The fact that we keep asking that question suggests we all agree we need to draw some lines and that the lines seem pretty blurry to most. If you're pursuing marriage, and it's going well, you're going to experience temptation—a lot of temptation and more all the time. Sexual sin may be the Devil's weapon of choice in corrupting Christian relationships. If we don't acknowledge our enemy and engage him, we'll find ourselves wondering how we lost so easily. Some of our best friends in the battle will be the boundaries we set to keep us pure.

While spontaneous plunges into intimacy look great in chick flicks and feel great in the moment, they breed shame, regret, and distrust. Let's try talking about touching before touching. Trade some titillation for trust, surprise for clarity and confidence. Make decisions prayerfully and intentionally before diving in. Boundaries are necessary, because on the road to marriage and its consummation, the appetite for intimacy only grows as you feed it. We are biologically built that way. Touching leads to more touching. Being alone together in certain situations welcomes overwhelming temptation. Even praying together or talking for hours upon hours on the phone can create unhealthy and premature overdoses of intimacy.

If we're honest, we much more often like to err by wading into love too far rather than waiting too long to take the next step. You will be hard-pressed, though, to find a married couple regretting the boundaries they made in dating, while you will very easily find those that wish they had made more. As followers of Christ, we really ought to be the most careful and vigilant. Boundaries protect, and boundaries provide the trenches of trust building. As we establish some mutual boundaries, small and large, and commit to keeping them together, we develop depths and patterns of trust that will serve our intimacy, covenant keeping, and decision making, should God lead us to marry. We will talk more about sexual purity in chapter 13 and about boundaries in chapter 14.

8. Consistently include your community.

Dating is a matter of doing your best to discern a person's ability to fulfill God's vision and purpose for marriage with you. While you might be the one with the final say, you might not be the best person to assess at every point. Just as in every other area of our Christian life, we need the body of Christ as we think about whom to date, how to date, and when to wed. While it's rarely quick or convenient, gaining the perspective of people who know us, love us, and have great hope for our future will always pay dividends. It may lead to hard conversations or deep disagreement, but it will force us to deal with things we did not or could not have seen on our own. We'll find safety with an abundance of counselors (Prov. 11:14). Invite other people to look into your relationship. Spend time together with other people, couples and singles, who are willing to point out the good, the bad, and the ugly. We'll talk more about community and accountability in chapter 15.

9. *Let all your dating be missionary dating.*

No, I am not encouraging you to date not-yet-believing men or women. When I say missionary dating, I mean dating that displays and promotes faith in Jesus and his good news, a dating that is in step with the gospel before the watching world. I want us to win disciples by dating radically, by confronting the world's paradigms and pleasure seeking with sacrifice, selflessness, and intentionality. Men and women in the world want many of the same things you want: affection, commitment, conversation, stability, and sex. And eventually they will see that the ground under your lives and relationship is firmer than the flimsy flings they've known. They'll see something deeper, stronger, and more meaningful between you and your significant other.

Do the people in each of your lives know and love Jesus more because you're together? Do they see God's grace and truth working in you and your relationship as you walk through life together? Are the two of you thinking proactively about how to bless your friends and family and point them to Christ? More and more, as the world is watering down dating, your relationship can be a provocative picture of your fidelity to Christ and a call to follow him.

While you wait and date, hope in Jesus more than marriage. Make it true first. Spend lots of time satisfying your soul in all that God has become for you in Jesus. Then be bold to say it, when all anyone wants to talk about is your love life. "So, any women in your life these days?" "Are the two of you an item?" "She's a really great girl. What do you think about her?" "Would you be willing to go on a date with my wife's cousin's roommate's brother?" Married people have lines, too. Use the awkward small talk as an opportunity to point *them* to the Groom who purchased your eternal happiness whether in life or in death, in sickness or in health, whether in matrimony or "on the market."

A Chance to Date Differently

Is this kind of dating perfectly safe? No. Will it keep you from being hurt or disappointed? No. Will it guarantee you never go through another breakup? No. But, by God's grace, it may guard you from deeper heartache and more devastating failure. My prayer is that these principles would prepare you to love your boyfriend or girlfriend (and your future spouse) in a way that more beautifully and dramatically displays the truth and power of the gospel. If you are like me, you may have blown it on multiple fronts already. Maybe you're blowing it right now. Be willing to make the hard decisions, large and small, to pursue marriage the right way today. Whether you're ultimately married to each other or not (or married at all, for that matter), you will thank each other later.

10

The Best Book on Dating

The single greatest book on the market today about dating wasn't written in the last year or even in the last ten years. It was written over the course of a thousand years and published more than two thousand years ago. It never mentions dating, or really anything even remotely like it. And it is still the best book on dating you can buy.

Some of you will be tempted to skip the chapter on the Bible to read about where to set physical boundaries or when to break up with your boyfriend. We're all prone to settle for simple, practical guidelines for life—just tell me what to do and when to do it—instead of constantly searching for deeper reasons to live and do everything we do. And because we settle for less, we often miss most of what the Bible has to offer. The Bible is not a textbook we shelve after we graduate from Sunday school, but a well of living water we need every new day. Jesus says, "If you *abide in my word*, you are truly my disciples" (John 8:31). We picture the Bible being stale and expired, when, in reality, it "is living and active, sharper than any two-edged sword, piercing to the division of soul and of spirit, of joints and of marrow, and discerning the thoughts and intentions of the heart" (Heb. 4:12). It's not a heavy anchor holding us from afar but a living and intimate friend for every decision and season of life.

New books on relationships and dating are being published all the time (including this one), but all of them combined cannot offer us what we already have in the Bible. If I can convince you to believe that, it will dramatically change how you live, read, and date. It might, for instance, make you more fascinated with Philippians than with the latest article being passed around Facebook. It might make you more likely to spend ten extra minutes each night reading Proverbs instead of ten more minutes watching Netflix. It could finally give you the courage to wake up a little earlier and start meditating on Scripture each morning.

Many of us let the Bible sit like a statue on our shelf because we think it has very little to do with our everyday lives. Things have changed over time, so we think we need new advice. We think voices today have a better perspective and better things to say about today simply because they're living in it. The Bible had its day, and we're grateful for it. We even kept a copy as a statue. We want volume 2. Or probably more like volume 2,000. But all we really need, for whatever decision, situation, or relationship we face this year, is the first and only volume of its kind: God's Word.

Is Dating Even in the Bible?

Perhaps the clearest statement in the Bible about what the Bible has to say about dating was written by Paul in a letter to his friend Timothy:

> But as for you, continue in what you have learned and have firmly believed, knowing from whom you learned it and how from childhood you have been acquainted with the sacred writings, which are able to make you wise for salvation through faith in Christ Jesus. All Scripture is breathed out by

God and profitable for teaching, for reproof, for correction, and for training in righteousness, that the man of God may be complete, equipped for every good work. (2 Tim. 3:14–17)

Paul doesn't say anything explicitly about dating—or marriage, or even friendship. But he does say something powerful about the Bible. First, the Bible solves our greatest problem. Then it tells us how to live. The Bible saves us—making us "wise for salvation through faith in Christ Jesus." It solves our greatest problem by bringing us the greatest news. "You were *dead* in the trespasses and sins in which you once walked" (Eph. 2:1–2). And then, one day, you weren't anymore. You believed and came alive. You might tell that story a thousand different ways, but God says you were saved with words—by "hearing through the word of Christ" (Rom. 10:17). We all are saved by God with words from God.

But God was not simply out to save us when he wrote the Bible. Paul goes on to say, "*All* Scripture is breathed out by God and profitable for teaching, for reproof, for correction, and for training in righteousness, that the man of God may be complete, equipped for *every* good work" (2 Tim. 3:16–17). *All* of Scripture is meant by God for *every* good work—every good decision, every act of self-control, every demonstration of Christlike love, anything we do to bring God glory (1 Cor. 10:31). God gave us a two-thousand-year-old book to tell us how to live today. He could have done it a million other ways, but he chose to write a book.

Dating is not a word you will find in your Bible. People did not date in Jesus's day. There's no Greek or Hebrew word for it buried in Deuteronomy or Psalms or Romans. If we read it cover to cover, we might easily come to the conclusion that this book has absolutely nothing to say about dating, but it says a *lot* about how we should relate to one another, and specifically about how men and women relate to one another.

Peter says the same thing a little differently when he writes,

"His divine power has granted to us *all things that pertain to life and godliness*, through the knowledge of him who called us to his own glory and excellence, by which he has granted to us his precious and very great promises" (2 Pet. 1:3–4). Before you scroll through social media or read the next blog or buy the next book, do you really believe that God has *already* given you "all things that pertain to life"—including dating—"and godliness"? He has. And he has done so "*through* the knowledge of him," which includes "his precious and very great promises." He has done so with the Bible—the only clear, undeniable way we know him and hear his promises. Even with sixty-six books and more than eight hundred thousand words, the Bible cannot speak *specifically* to everything every Christian will experience in this world throughout history. But it still promises to speak meaningfully to everything, including our pursuit of marriage.

A Dating Book about God

Paul says, "Whatever was written in former days was written for our instruction, that through endurance and through the encouragement of the Scriptures we might have hope" (Rom. 15:4; see also 1 Cor. 10:11). Books written hundreds of years before Christ were written for *our* instruction. Letters written in the first century were written for *our* hope. As the world ages and changes, there will always be more to say. If I didn't believe that, I wouldn't have written this book. But anything truly meaningful and helpful I have to say will be built on what is already in the Word. That means ultimately there's nothing original or new to say. God has told us how to live and how to love. Our job is to listen and listen and listen, and *then* maybe try to make sense of what it means today. People who read the Bible that way stand out in the world, and they make wise decisions in dating.

The Bible is a dating book about God. Or a business book about God. Or a biology book about God. The Bible is about

God. God created everything—mother giraffes, the Milky Way galaxy, and every marriage—and he alone gives each thing he has created its purpose and meaning. He's the author of the world (every creature in every corner), the author of the Bible, and the author and perfecter of our faith (Heb. 1:1–2; 12:2), who, with his Word and his Spirit, gives us everything we need to do his will. Therefore, the Bible is a [fill-in-the-blank] book about God. It's the world's one definitive book about everything, the book against which every other book should be measured and judged (including this one). I hope you are reading *Not Yet Married* with your Bibles open, "examining the Scriptures" to see if the things I am saying are so (see Acts 17:11).

Some "Outdated" Dating Advice

It's one thing to suggest that the Bible is profitable and another thing to prove it, so I want to look together at one really old story in the Bible, as an exercise, and ask if it has anything to say for twenty-first-century dating. Applying some parts of Scripture to dating will obviously be more difficult than others, but I want you to see that through prayer and the help of the Holy Spirit, the hard work is possible and worth it. We will look at Genesis 24. Marriage and dating are *not* the main point of that chapter, but that doesn't mean we can't learn something about marriage and dating from the story. If you have time, it might be good to reread the chapter for yourself before reading what God has shown me.

The first thing in the Bible even remotely resembling today's dating scene might be the marriage between Isaac and Rebekah. Lots of people were married before Isaac and Rebekah, but we don't read about anyone *getting* married. Well, except in the garden, and I think we can all agree that the situation (and surgery) in that case was extraordinary. In Genesis 24 Abraham, Isaac's father, sends a servant to Abraham's hometown to find a wife for his son. Rebekah gives the servant's camels a drink, he gives her a couple of heavy bracelets, her family approves, she meets Isaac for the first time at a tent—and they're married. Forget love at first sight. Their story is lifelong covenant at first sight.

If you've wanted to be married and aren't, you might read Genesis 24 (as strange as it may seem today) with at least a little bit of curiosity and even longing—it just seems so simple and clean. After dating off and on for fourteen years, I know I did. If you think about it any longer, though, you'll probably dismiss their story as ancient and outdated, as irrelevant for twenty-first-century Christians. The Old Testament may not be prescriptive when it comes to dating, but it is certainly profitable. Don't (necessarily) go buying a couple of camels and some heavy bracelets. Certainly don't marry a woman and her sister (see Jacob, Leah, and Rachel in Genesis 29). But if you slow down and pray enough, you might see things in "outdated" parts of the Bible that you can apply on the way to your wedding day. Following are five I found in Isaac and Rebekah's story.

1. Put the pressure on God and not yourself.

When Abraham commissioned his servant to find a wife for Isaac, the servant worried that a woman might not go for the whole arranged-marriage-to-a-man-in-a-faraway-land idea. Abraham responds,

> The LORD . . . who spoke to me and swore to me, "To your offspring I will give this land," *he will send his angel before you,* and you shall take a wife for my son from there. (Gen. 24:7)

The longer you long to be married and aren't, the more likely you are to think the problem is with you, that you have to change or try something new. God may be revealing that to you, or he might simply want you to wait while *he* works. There's really only one worker in the wedding industry. While the servant ran ahead to find a woman in Mesopotamia, God went ahead of him to do the real work that Isaac and Rebekah needed. Moses writes, "The [servant] gazed at [Rebekah] in silence to learn whether *the* LORD had prospered his journey or not" (Gen. 24:21). God not only joins a husband and a wife (Matt. 19:6), but he brings them to each other. If you're mainly looking to yourself to get married, you've put the pressure in the wrong place.

2. Pursue him or her with an open hand.

Before Abraham let the servant proceed on his mission, he gave him clear instructions and ended by saying, "If the woman is not willing to follow you, then you will be free from this oath of mine" (Gen. 24:8). Abraham believed God would provide a wife for his son. And yet he held out open hands before God: "If the Lord wills," my son will have a wife, and my servant will find her on this journey (see James 4:15). Until you say your vows at the altar, know that God may write a different wedding story than you would write for yourself. And with all his wisdom, power, and love, we have reason to praise him that he does.

3. Pray and pray and pray.

Before the servant saw a single woman, he prayed, "O LORD, God of my master Abraham, please grant me success today and show steadfast love to my master Abraham" (Gen. 24:12). When did you start praying for a spouse? When did you stop? We love when our prayers are answered in twenty-four hours. What if God withholds what we want for a year? Or ten? Or more? God doesn't want us to take anything for granted in this life, certainly not our spouse. He wants all the glory in giving us what's best for us whenever he gives it to us. If we desire a husband or wife, we should love casting our anxiety and longing on the one who cares for us (1 Pet. 5:7; see also Phil. 4:6–7). Don't start dating without praying, and don't stop praying while you're waiting.

4. Look to loved ones for confirmation.

Let the people around you who love you confirm he or she is the one. Abraham's servant explains to her father (Bethuel) and brother (Laban) all that's happened and why he believes she might be the one to marry Isaac.

> Then Laban and Bethuel answered and said, "The thing has come from the LORD; we cannot speak to you bad or good. Behold, Rebekah is before you; take her and go, and let her be the wife of your master's son, as the LORD has spoken." (Gen. 24:50–51)

If God has brought the two of you together, he will make it clear to other believers in your life. If people who love you and follow Jesus have serious reservations about your relationship, *you* should probably have serious reservations too. Don't rely only on your own instincts (or your significant other's) to give you confidence that he or she is the one. Infatuation in dating relationships will blind and deafen you to things you would never miss in other relationships. Trust God enough to listen to other believers in your life.

5. Date for more than marriage.

Finally, if you're single and want to be married, marriage can begin to feel like the goal of your life, your own long-awaited promised land. Said another way, we're prone to idolize marriage while dating, resting our hope and happiness on him or her rather than on God. How did Abraham's servant react when God brought him the right woman?

> The man bowed his head and worshiped the LORD and said, "Blessed be the LORD, the God of my master Abraham, who has not forsaken his steadfast love and his faithfulness toward my master. As for me, the LORD has led me in the way to the house of my master's kinsmen." (Gen. 24:26–27; see v. 48)

The servant saw through Rebekah to God, and he worshiped. Worship is the goal of all Christian dating, because worship is the goal of the Christian life. God did not make us to be married but to make much of him. Marriage is about knowing God, worshiping God, depending on God, displaying God, and being made like God. If our dating—any given night out or a decade of trying—ends in marriage and not worship, it will ultimately be empty and unsatisfying. Date for more than marriage.

As we finish Genesis 24, you can hear the wedding bells: "Then Isaac brought her into the tent of Sarah his mother and took Rebekah, and she became his wife, and he loved her" (Gen. 24:67). God's name doesn't appear in this verse, but by this time you should hear it anyway: God did this. God gave this woman to this man, and this man to this woman. From beginning to end, and everywhere in between, God was working, and he rewarded those who waited for him (Isa. 64:4). It all happens so fast here in Genesis 24 that it can feel even more foreign to those of us today who have waited for years and years to be married. The story of Isaac and Rebekah, though, is not about how immediately the answer came, but that the answer and the marriage came from God. At every step in your pursuit of marriage, look to God, every person's hope for true happiness and the author of every Christian love story.

Think Over What God Says

We can learn a lot from Isaac and Rebekah's story, but we're not limited to Genesis 24 when reading the Bible for dating advice. We learn patience from Jacob, who waited seven years for his girl (Gen. 29:20)—and then seven more (29:28). Judges shows us the consequences of doing what seems right in our own eyes (Judg. 21:25)—doing what's comfortable in the moment or common in our society. David's story warns us that sin, especially sexual sin, will be enticing (2 Sam. 11:3), and it will abuse us and everyone else involved (2 Sam. 11:17; 12:18). Proverbs is filled with wisdom for dating relationships—counsel for developing good communication, choosing a spouse, resisting sexual temptation, and much more. Those are all examples before Jesus, who is the perfect picture of and model for loving others.

The Bible was written more for us than we often realize. Reading and applying the Bible to dating will not be easy, but it will be worth it. God himself promises to read *with* us. But we have to be willing to put in the time and wait for him to speak. Paul says, "Think over what I say, for *the Lord* will give you understanding in everything" (2 Tim. 2:7). As we slow down and think about what God has said, he will reveal more and more of what it means for us. Does that make you want to read the Bible again? Does it make you wonder how much you missed that might address what you're facing right now? I hope so. If you give your life to reading that book, it will reward you far more than it will ever cost you.

11

Your Last First Date

It was our first date. I wasn't even completely sure she knew it was a date. We met at a wedding and then talked on the phone once a week or so for a couple of months. I asked if I could take her out, and she conceded. I bought a couple of board games, chose a trendy new taco joint, and found a nonchain coffee shop to hang out in after lunch. Coffee said I'm interested and serious but not desperate. Board games said I know how to laugh and have fun, but I'm here to win. I don't know what tacos said, but I like them.

It was a great date (at least from where I was sitting). The restaurant was everything I had hoped for—a casual and upbeat atmosphere but quiet enough to talk and get to know each other. The food was unique and delicious but not too heavy. She was impressed. We played games at the coffee shop all afternoon. I let her win enough to make sure she had a good time. Okay, maybe she just beat me more than I expected. Either way, we had a lot of fun. And the conversation was a sweet mixture of serious and silly, of storytelling and good follow-up questions, all of it filled with our shared love for Jesus. A few hours went by really fast.

We came to the end of the afternoon. Excited and confident, I decided to put myself out there: "I had a really great time today, and I've really enjoyed getting to know you over the last couple of months. I don't know what you're feeling"—well, I was pretty sure I *did* know—"but I'd love if we could get to know each other more in a relationship."

She smiled. My heart jumped through the new shirt I had bought the day before. "I had a great time today too." she said.

It was pretty great, wasn't it?

"And I've really enjoyed getting to know you too."

I knew it.

"I've really enjoyed the conversations I've had with you, and the way you've pointed me to Jesus."

Sounds like boyfriend material.

"You've become a really good friend."

Uh-oh.

"You're a nice human being . . ."

Wait, what does that even mean?

". . . but when I think about a relationship, my heart is cold."

Long, awkward, uncomfortable pause. "Cold?"

"Yeah, cold."

"Like ice-cold or a little lukewarm?"

"Cold."

What went so wrong? What should I have done differently? It all seemed so comfortable, so exciting, so right, so sure. But when the day was done, she was colder than a Dairy Queen, and I was just a "nice human being." It had started to feel like this might finally be my last first date. Of course, I guess first dates had felt like that before. Either way, here I was, back where I began. Roller-coaster rides like these were enough to make me want to give up on marriage.

Can Marriage Really Be Worth It?

"Maybe marriage isn't all that great after all."

When divorce rates are high and the surviving marriages around us seem broken, messy, and unhappy—and when there *are* plenty of other good things to keep us busy—lots of young men and women in their twenties and thirties have basically given up on marriage, or at least we've discounted it in our plans and dreams. Some of us have tried dating and been burned—confusion, rejections, sexual failure, breakups, or whatever else plagues our relationships. With all the pain, failure, and friction, it simply can't be worth it, can it? There are other ways for me to be known and loved. Marriage isn't necessary for my happiness or significance here on earth.

That last sentence is true and important, but I fear our generation might be overlooking some significant things about what marriage really *is* and why, at least for many, it's worth all the time, patience, and even heartache. Lots of not-yet-married people need to be reminded that marriage is spectacular and needed in our society, and that's because it belongs to God. The beauty of marriage far surpasses the functional, social, relational, and, yes, even the sexual benefits. For believers in Jesus, the importance and allure of matrimony ought to be deeply spiritual, missional, and eternal.

Two thousand years ago, people were already questioning whether marriage was worth it. Paul says, "Some will depart from the faith by devoting themselves to deceitful spirits and teachings of demons" (1 Tim. 4:1). What lies were they believing when they left the faith? What were the demons saying? They *"forbid marriage* and require abstinence from foods that God created to be received with thanksgiving by those who believe and know the truth" (1 Tim. 4:3). When we forget the goodness and beauty of marriage, we forget something good and beautiful *God* is doing in the world. Why? "For everything created *by God*"—including marriage and every kind of food—"is good, and nothing is to be rejected if it is received with thanksgiving" (1 Tim. 4:4). God made marriage, and he meant for lots of Christians to marry and to enjoy marriage with thankful hearts. He calls it *good*, even today. To say otherwise is to say something about him.

Some of us have given up on marriage because it doesn't seem all that great anymore. Others have given up because we want it more than anything, and we're tired and beat up from trying to find it. We quietly, even subconsciously, moved marriage ahead of God on our wish list, so we're often miserable while we wait around for our husband or wife. But until we have found our happiness, significance, and belonging in the right places, we'll never be ready to be married.

Do you want to know why there are so many divorces, even among Christians? In part, it's because so many people have tried to find ultimate happiness, significance, or ultimate belonging in the arms of a man or a woman. Marriage seemed like the answer for a while—a few years, a few months, a few minutes even—then it fell short. It left them wanting, even demanding, more from marriage, not seeing that their demands were too much for marriage. They blamed their emptiness, loneliness, and joylessness on marriage instead of seeing that it was never meant to satisfy their deepest needs. There are lots of bad reasons to get married, and the worst is that we think he or she could be what only God can be for us.

Your Wedding Is Still Something Worth Wanting

If we give up on marriage but love dating, something has gone seriously wrong. All our desires for dating should spring from a big vision of what marriage is and why it's worth wanting. With every date, we should have our last first date in mind. Marriage is the only thing big enough, strong enough, and worth enough for all the risks we take in dating. If you're tempted to give up on marriage or discount it, don't let worldly trends convince you marriage is a small and unnecessary accessory to be added on later in the full and happy life. Before you pour yourself deeper and deeper into your career or your favorite hobby instead of pursuing marriage, consider these five reasons your wedding might still be something worth wanting.

1. When God made the world, marriage was a critical part of his perfect creation.

There was a day—or at least a few hours—when marriage was pure, undefiled, free from all sin and selfishness. In fact, the whole world was that way. God had looked on his creation, and it was good—complete, flawless, rich, and filled with life (Gen. 1:31). And a central part of that truly utopian world was marriage—a man and a woman joined together as one in a God-ordained, God-filled, and God-glorifying union (Gen. 1:27). Marriage wasn't an optional or incidental arrangement in God's agenda. It was right there at the center, tying together the two most significant characters in this new and epic story.

For sure, sin has broken and marred what was once good and pure about marriage. But Paul quotes Genesis 2 (before sin came into the picture) and says that *from the very beginning*, the mystery of marriage is that it was meant to represent Jesus's relationship with the church. "'Therefore a man shall leave his father and mother and hold fast to his wife, and the two shall become one flesh.' This mystery is profound, and I am saying that it refers to Christ and the church" (Eph. 5:31–32). This means sin wasn't a surprise in God's design for marriage. Rather, it tragically, but really beautifully, served to fulfill God's reasons for making marriage. Marriages today, though flawed, are still carrying out, though imperfectly, the glorious purposes God gave them in the garden.

2. Christian marriages expose ignorant, shortsighted priorities in our society.

Individualism, consumerism, and careerism have cheapened the perceived value and centrality of marriage. It's now more often viewed as simply a convenient social accessory to a person's other dreams and ambitions. And it's regularly (and sadly) evaluated, and even ended, based on whether it's serving our other aspirations. We are happy to be married if it's making us happy and helping us accomplish our goals. If it gets difficult or boring, slows us down, or requires more of us, we just withdraw, punish our spouse and kids (directly or indirectly), and eventually get out and cut our losses. Unless, of course, Jesus is the point of our marriages and the power to sustain them.

Anyone who has experienced marriage will testify that it's hard. That has been true across generations, cultures, and worldviews. Marriages never survive for decades on comfort and self-fulfillment, at least not happily. Marriages endure and thrive on unchanging, selfless mutual commitment to each other and to something bigger, stronger, and longer lasting than the marriage. Christian marriage, therefore, is an opportunity to show the world something—even better, to show them *someone*—strong enough to keep a marriage together and make it unbelievably meaningful and happy.

3. Children are a miracle, and God means for us to bear and raise children in marriage.

Bearing or adopting children is not the only way to bring people to faith in Jesus Christ, but it's proven again and again in history to be one of the most effective. You will have a natural, unusual, and God-given authority and influence over your kids. Marriage gives you the unique ability to structure their growth, speak into their hearts, and model God's hope and love. And they are a miracle, every one of them. Every new person—formed and sustained by God in the mother's womb—is a stunning miracle (Ps. 139:13).

Children are a miracle worth making, which means they are a miracle worth planning and sacrificing for. Future generations of men and women will run the world, the church, and your local neighborhood. Who will those future men and women be? What kinds of homes will they experience? What lessons will they learn at age four, and twelve, and fifteen? When will they hear about Jesus? Who will be the Christian examples in their lives? It's difficult to overestimate the lasting productivity and treasure of bearing children and training them to be men and women after God. Of course, there are other ways—countless other ways—to invest in raising up future generations of young people. You can teach. You can mentor. You can support other parents. But nothing really replaces the lifelong, every-moment relationship, commitment, and responsibility of having them in your home, under your roof and care.

4. Marriage is one of God's most effective ways of making us like Jesus.

This one is admittedly inspired more by personal testimony than by any one quote from the Bible, but it's also fair to say it's a commonsense conclusion. If you put two God-fearing, Jesus-following, but sinful people in such close proximity, with a covenant to keep them from running away, there will be tension, conflict, and *hopefully* change. Perhaps the greatest means God has given us, under the Holy Spirit, for making us more like himself are the people in our lives who love us enough to confront our patterns of selfishness, unhealthiness, and sin. Marriage places that loving person right next to us in the same family, the same house, the same budget, and the same promises. Tim Keller writes:

> God loved us, not because we were lovely to him, but to make us lovely. . . . Each spouse should see the great thing that Jesus is doing in the life of their mate through the Word, the gospel. Each spouse then should give him- or herself to be a vehicle for that work and envision the day that you stand together before God, seeing each other presented in spotless beauty and glory. . . . Romance, sex, laughter, and plain fun are

the by-products of this process of sanctification, refinement, glorification.[7]

5. Marriage declares the gospel as consistently and clearly as any other relationship.

God's counsel for marriage is cross-shaped. The path to the most beautiful, most powerful, most satisfying marriages is the road to Calvary. The Bible is clear that the behaviors and rhythms of the marriage covenant are a billboard for Christ's forgiving, sacrificial, redeeming love for sinners. Paul repeats this in several ways, speaking to husbands and wives:

> The husband is the head of the wife even as Christ is the head of the church, his body, and is himself *its Savior*. (Eph. 5:23)

> Husbands, love your wives, as Christ loved the church and *gave himself up for her*. (Eph. 5:25)

> "Therefore a man shall leave his father and mother and hold fast to his wife, and the two shall become one flesh." This mystery is profound, and I am saying that it refers to *Christ and the church*. (Eph. 5:31–32)

You rarely see this kind of Christlike love in other relationships, because the stakes are never as high. A husband and wife have covenanted before *God* to love each other until *death*. There are no exit ramps or escape hatches. That might sound scary to some, but we were made for this kind of love—covenantal, enduring, lavish, promise-keeping love. It's how God loves us, and it's the kind of love that parades—tangibly and consistently—the gospel of grace, hope, and forgiveness before our needy world.

Are You Called to Marry?

Now, marriage is not for everyone. We've seen already that the Bible is wonderfully clear on that matter (see 1 Cor. 7:8). God has lovingly and specifically called, set apart, equipped, and sent lots of unmarried men and women into the world for a lifetime of bearing witness to the satisfying sufficiency of his Son—to tell the world you don't have to be married to be happy. But even those called and commissioned by God to a life of singleness have every reason to celebrate Christian marriage—every living, breathing, and believing image of Christ's love for his church.

How do you know you're called to marry? Well, you don't until you do (at least not for sure). Plenty of people have felt called to be a doctor, a musical artist, or a professional basketball player, but that calling doesn't become real until they get their license, take the stage, or sign the big contract. We'll look at this more in the next several chapters, but a calling to marriage might be more complicated than we think. It's not just a matter of whether we've wanted to marry since before we were teenagers. We may feel a deep desire and *sense* of calling to marriage, but that's only one piece of the puzzle. That calling should be confirmed in community with other believers who love us, and who love Jesus. Our calling can also be confirmed by whether God gives us the opportunity to date someone, and then by whether he confirms the same sense of calling in his or her heart and community. Until all those pieces come together, we shouldn't assume we're called to marry or that we're *not* called to singleness. In the end, we can't be sure we're called to marriage until we marry.

What about singleness? Until we marry (if we do), we are called to singleness. A calling to singleness is as real and significant as any call to marriage. It's not a default calling. God does not do default callings. A calling, by definition, is intentional and personal, not passive and sweeping. But unlike a calling to marriage, a calling to singleness is never necessarily set in stone. Once we marry, we are called to be married till death do us part. No take-backs or trades. If God calls us to singleness, he may call us to singleness for the rest of our life—he does that for many—or he may call us to singleness for a season (five years, ten years, maybe even fifty years) before calling us to marry.

A Love Declared, Not Discovered

If God does call us to marry, we will have to relearn how to love. The beauty and joy of Christian marriage is not compatibility. That feels like the rare jewel we're hunting for in all our dating relationships, but relationships and marriages don't stand out or last because the two of us make sense together. No, the beauty and joy of Christian marriage is Christ, shining in our joyful and unwavering commitment to each other, even when we're least compatible and least deserving of each other's love. Keller says, "Wedding vows are not a declaration of present love but a mutually binding promise of future love."[8] Marriage is mainly a love declared, not a love discovered. Have you thought about your wedding day that way? The promises you will make before God, and before all your friends and family, have almost nothing to do with what you experienced and enjoyed in your dating relationship, and everything to do with the uncertain and uncontrollable months and years ahead. You're not standing there together to say, "I really do love you," but to say instead, "I really *will* love you"—whatever it takes, however hard it gets, whatever happens, however much I want to leave. That kind of love will stand out in the world, and it will last long after many have given up and walked away.

The best marriages will be the hardest to explain—not because you are so different (you might be), but because you're still loving each other so patiently, sacrificially, and passionately after years of inconvenience, conflict, and sacrificing so much. How do they still love each other so much? Well, because we have been loved like that and more. Paul says, "*While we were still weak*, at the right time Christ died for the ungodly. . . . God shows his love for us in that *while we were still sinners*, Christ died for us" (Rom. 5:6–8).

He didn't die for us because he finally found the love of his life. We were not marriage material when he met us. No, he died to make us the love of his life despite how little we deserved him. A love like his makes a marriage worth wanting, and it makes a marriage worth keeping—a love declared, not discovered.

In all your dating, keep your last first date in mind. I definitely didn't know it at the time, but mine was over trendy tacos, coffee, and board games. The Dairy Queen slowly warmed over the next few months. She became my girlfriend that May, and then my wife almost two years later. Over those two years in between, we kept a big, sacred, breathtaking picture of marriage in front of us. We had no idea if we would get married, and we never assumed we would. In fact, we intentionally dated as if we were going to marry someone else, to keep us from idolizing each other or going too far too soon. But we knew the only thing worth dating for was a marriage—a lifelong, life-on-life love like Jesus's love for us. Nothing else was worth all the risk we took when we began to share our heart with someone else. Nothing else would protect us from diving in too quickly or jumping ship when things got hard. Nothing else would stand out enough from the world around us to say something significant about Jesus. Marriage had to be the big and beautiful goal of our dating before we were ever ready to date well.

12

Is He the One?

In some ways, I wrote the second half of this book so that I could write this chapter. It's not necessarily the most important chapter—it might be for you—but it's the chapter I wanted to write the most. I got lots of things wrong in dating, but as I think back over my mistakes and failures—dating too young, jumping from relationship to relationship, not being honest with myself or with others, failing to set boundaries or to keep the ones I did, not listening to my friends and family, not prizing and pursuing purity—one rises above the others and in many ways explains the others: my dating relationships were mainly a pursuit of intimacy, not clarity.

In my best moments, I was pursuing clarity *through* intimacy, but in a lot of other moments, if I'm honest, I just wanted intimacy at whatever cost. "The pursuit of marriage" was a warm and justifying pullover to wear over my conscience when things started to go too far. But even clarity *through* intimacy misses the point and gets it backwards. I should have been pursuing clarity *and then* intimacy. That simple equation would have saved me and the girls I dated all kinds of grief, heartache, and regret.

Most of us date because we want intimacy. We want to feel

close to someone. We want to be known deeply and loved deeply. We want sex. We want to share life with a man or woman—someone who will be involved and invested in what we're doing and what we care about. With the right heart and in the right measure and at the right time, these are all good desires. God made many of us to want these things and therefore wants us to want these things—with the right heart, in the right measure, and at the right time.

Think about your last first kiss in a relationship (if you've already kissed someone). Why did you do it? You knew you were risking something, that this wasn't the safest way to give yourself to someone. What was driving you most in those brief moments before you let your lips touch his (or hers)? For me, every first kiss was driven more by my own desires than by God's desires for me—every first kiss until I kissed my wife for the first time, seconds after asking her to be my wife. Before Faye, I had let what I wanted outweigh what I knew God wanted and what I knew was best for the girl I was dating. I craved intimacy, and I knew I would find it in marriage. So I punched "marriage" into Google Maps, jumped on the highway, and ignored the speed limits. Instead of waiting to get to my destination to enjoy emotional and sexual intimacy, I pulled over and bought something quicker and cheaper on the side of the road.

Intimacy—romantic or otherwise—is a beautiful and precious gift God has given to his children. But like so many of God's good gifts, because of our sin, intimacy is also very dangerous. The human heart is wired to want intimacy, but it is also wired to corrupt intimacy—to demand intimacy in the wrong ways or at the wrong time, and to expect the wrong things from intimacy. That means intimacy between sinners is dangerous, because we're prone, by nature, to hurt one another—to do what feels good instead of caring for the other person; to promise too much too soon instead of being patient and slow to speak; to put our hope, identity, and worth in one another instead of in God. Intimacy makes us vulnerable, and sin makes us dangerous. The two together, without covenant promises, are a formula for disaster in dating.

Different Prizes in Marriage and Dating

We've already established that God—not each other, not love, not sex, not friendship—makes marriage worth having. God is the great benefit for every believer, at whatever age, in whatever stage of life, and whatever their marital status. But is there a unique prize for the believer in marriage? Yes, it is Christ-centered emotional and sexual intimacy with another believer. Before God, within the covenant of marriage, two lives, two hearts, two bodies become *one*. A husband and wife experience everything in life as *one* new person. "Couple" doesn't describe them sufficiently anymore. Yes, they're still themselves, but they're too close now to ever be separated again (Mark 10:9). God has made them one. Their things are not their own. Their time is not their own. Even their bodies are not their own (1 Cor. 7:4). They share all and enjoy all *together* now. Sex is the intense experience and picture of their new union, but it's only a small slice of all the intimacy they enjoy together now.

The reason that kind of intimacy is the prize of marriage and *not* of our not-yet-married relationships is that this kind of intimacy is never safe anywhere outside of a covenant. *Never.* There are lots of contexts in which romantic intimacy *feels* safe outside of marriage, but it never is. There is too much at stake with our hearts and too many risks involved without a ring. Without promises before God, the further we walk into intimacy with a man or woman, the further we expose ourselves to the possibility of being abandoned, betrayed, and crushed. In a Christ-centered *marriage*, those same risks do not exist. We are together—in sickness and health, in peace and conflict, in disappointment, tragedy, and even failure—until death do us part. When God unites us, death is the only thing strong enough to separate us. That means intimacy is a safe and appropriate experience *in marriage*. For sure, it's not perfectly safe. Married people are still sinful people, meaning they're still capable of hurting one another, even to the point of abuse or divorce. But faithful married people are not leaving people. Just like God is not a leaving God.

If we want to have and enjoy such Christ-centered intimacy, we need to get married. And if we want to get married, we need to pursue clarity about whom to marry. We don't pursue clarity by diving into intimacy. The right kind of clarity is a means to the right kind of intimacy, not the other way around. Careful, prayerful, thoughtful clarity will produce healthy, lasting, passionate intimacy. Any other road to intimacy will sabotage it, leaving it shallow, fragile, and unreliable.

Bicycles and Airplanes

A lot of the heartache and confusion we feel in dating stems from treating dating mainly as practice for marriage (clarity *through* intimacy), instead of as discernment toward marriage (clarity *and then* intimacy). In dating, we experiment with intimacy until it basically feels like marriage, and then we get married. The risks seem worth it (even necessary), because of how much we want to be married (or at least everything that comes with being married). But the risks are not worth it, and they're certainly not necessary. God did not mean for us to risk so much in our pursuit of marriage. For sure, we always make ourselves vulnerable to some degree as we get to know someone and develop a relationship, but God wants us to enjoy intimacy *mainly* (almost exclusively) within a covenant, not in some science lab of love. In Christian dating, we're not trying marriage on for size, but trying to find someone to marry.

We want marriage to be like riding a bike, but God intended it to be more like flying a plane. To earn your pilot's license, first you have to go to ground school and learn about aerodynamics, radio communications, aircraft systems, navigation, weather, federal aviation regulations, flight planning, emergency procedures and scenarios, and more. You have to do hours of supervised flying, in which you learn about preflight inspections, taxiing, pre-takeoff checks, wind patterns, different approach and landing techniques, and how to deal with malfunctions and emergencies. Once you have demonstrated consistency in takeoffs and landings, proficiency in certain flight maneuvers, and good judgment, the instructor approves you to fly solo. Even then, you're allowed only to take off and land the first few times you fly. Eventually, you will be allowed to fly in a restricted practice area. After more experience, you will be approved to fly from airport to airport. Then you'll take a test, and you *finally* might earn your license.

When we experiment with intimacy in dating, we hop in the plane and treat it like a bike. We skip the classes, the instructor, and the tests, and just wing it. Why are we so ready to be so reckless? Because we crave intimacy, often more than we even desire marriage. We want marriage to be more like riding a bike. If someone's there to coach us, great. If not, no worries. We will just keep trying and trying until something feels right and we're able to ride. The scraped knees or bruised arms hurt, but they're just the price we pay to learn, right? No, we should not practice ourselves into marriage, risking bruised and broken hearts. There's too much at stake to throw ourselves into intimacy, even with the right training wheels. Dating is not junior varsity marriage. It's not a scrimmage. In dating, we do learn a lot in preparation for marriage, but it would be dangerous to treat dating like it's some lesser, experimental form of marriage. Instead of experimenting with marriage, we should be pursuing clarity about marriage.

How Do You Know?

Most people pursue clarity about dating from within their own heart. How do *I* feel about this person? Am *I* ready for this relationship to move forward? Do *I* want to marry this person? There are at least two other dimensions, however, to a healthy sense of clarity (think height, width, and depth): confirmation from our *community* and (maybe more often overlooked, or at least taken for granted) the *opportunity* to pursue or marry someone. We'll look more at the community's role in clarity in chapter 15, and I'll address the opportunity aspect of clarity briefly near the end of this chapter. But let's talk first about the clarity that happens in our own hearts. How do you know he (or she) is the one?

At its simplest, we are looking for someone we can marry. That answer will impress no one, but its simplicity carries a lot more weight than meets the eye. I hope you've seen that so far in the book. Marriage is not simply about sex, companionship, children, and tax benefits. We want our marriages (and our whole lives) to make Jesus *look* like our Lord, Savior, and treasure, because he *is* our Lord, Savior, and greatest treasure. We want our marriages to consistently and beautifully tell the story of the gospel, of God's patient, selfless, faithful love for sinners. We want our marriages to make us more like Christ, slowly but surely molding us into something new, different, and holy. When we look for someone we can marry, we're not looking first for something physical or financial or convenient or fun. We're looking for God in one another and in our future together.

One piece of the clarity we need in our own hearts is a personal, subjective sense of calling—a sense that our desire to get married to this person is a *good* desire that's a result of God's work in us rather than a bad desire that's yet to be redeemed and reshaped by God. We have to ask if we want to marry this person mainly because we want God, or if God is more of a distant relative in this dating relationship. David says, "Delight yourself *in the* LORD, and he will give you the desires of your heart" (Ps. 37:4). When God is our greatest joy—our greatest desire and greatest priority—we can begin to trust the desires of our hearts. If God always comes second, or third, or worse in our heart, then our desires cannot be trusted. As we date, we're looking for a settled sense of calling and conviction that this relationship is of God and that this marriage would be for God.

How do we know he (or she) is the one? First, you need to ask if *God* is the one. Do each of you love God more than you love each other? Your flesh will desperately *want* to be number one in your significant other's heart, but you need someone who won't let you have that spot. You need a husband or a wife who could be married to you for fifty years and still go to the grave loving Jesus more than you. Only then will he have the perspective to love you well, in dating and in marriage. He can do all kinds of things to make you feel good about yourself—tell you you're pretty, buy you all the things you want, do whatever, whenever to serve your wants or needs—but he cannot love you well unless you are not his first love. But if his love for you is an expression of his love for God, he will be supernaturally focused and equipped to love you in all the daily needs and circumstances of marriage.

Physical Attraction

So before he or she can be the one, God must be the one. How significant, then, should physical attraction be in the pursuit of clarity? Or, what role, if any, should physical appearance play in Christian dating? Different guys have come to me over the years asking about this. Usually he respects or admires a godly young woman (or, maybe more often, other people in his life think he *should* admire her more), and yet he's not physically attracted to her. She's not his type, he says, so he asks, "Should I still pursue her?"

I typically say no. Or, at least, not yet. Given the common assumptions and practices in our society today, including in the church, I do not believe a man (or woman) should begin a dating relationship with someone to whom he (or she) is not physically attracted. If he admires other things about her, I'm all for him *befriending* her and getting to know her in safe, unambiguous, nonflirtatious ways (probably in groups). But I believe physical attraction, at least in the vast majority of cases, is one critical piece in discerning whether to date or marry someone.

That being said, I also believe that physical attraction is far deeper and more dynamic, even spiritual, than we tend to think. It's not static or objective. Real, meaningful, durable attraction is far more than physical. So, for example, a woman's physical appearance plays only one role in what makes her attractive or appealing. Its role is massive initially, say, the very first time you see her, when all you know about her is what you see, before you even know her name or hear her voice. But its role will necessarily evolve the more you learn about her. After you've learned more—by asking her friends, hearing her talk, or watching the way she lives—you'll never see her again as just the person you saw at first. The more you learn about her, the more her appearance is filled, for better or for worse, with new and deeper meaning—with her personality, convictions, sense of humor, and faith. The once-stunning girl may lose most of her charm, and the easily overlooked girl may become undeniably beautiful. They each look exactly the same as before, and yet they don't. You see them, even their physical appearance, differently now.

Physical attraction is real but flexible. God has wired us to appreciate beauty in his design—to find people of the opposite gender physically appealing—and that is a real and important element in our pursuit of marriage and eventually in our flourishing within the covenant. God gave us physical senses and desires for our good. But mutual faith in Jesus Christ should be the most stunning and appealing thing about any potential spouse. "Charm is deceitful, and beauty is vain, but a woman who fears the LORD is to be praised" (Prov. 31:30). Why does Solomon even need to say that? Because physical beauty and charm are naturally appealing. But without faith, they're fading, and fast.

Christians should be cultivating hearts that are more attracted to faith and character than anything else. As godly men and women, we should find godliness incredibly attractive. In fact, in our eyes and hearts, it should be the most arrestingly attractive thing about the most attractive people. The world around us will preach that physical beauty is everything, but we know and desire better. Of all the people in the world, we should be the most free from enslavement to physical appearances and sexual titillation. As we put on the eyes and heart of Christ, we should increasingly be able to see through all the temporary and fading appearances to the things that are truly beautiful—the qualities in each other that imitate Jesus and anticipate heaven. The qualities that get better with age.[9]

God Will Make It Clear

Our hearts and even our community are not enough to give us the clarity we need. Our hearts will speak (calling), our friends will speak (community), and God will speak (opportunity). Really, God speaks in all three ways, but sometimes he speaks clearest in the last way. And yet we rarely stop to listen. You might fall in love with someone, and your friends and family may think it's a great idea, and it still may not happen. Maybe she doesn't like you back. She prefers just being friends. Maybe he dates and marries someone else. Maybe he moves away for school or work, and the distance feels too far for him. God does make his will clear by clarifying things in our hearts, but he also makes his will clear in other ways too. He creates an opportunity, or he takes one away. The Lord gives, and the Lord takes away (Job 1:21).

Does that sound cruel? Why would God give us a good desire for something (or someone), and then not give it to us? One of the most important things to learn about following Jesus is that there are a thousand good answers to that question. If God withholds something good from us, it's not because he wants to hurt us (Rom. 8:28). Never. It's because he wants what's best for us. Don't assume that a good desire confirmed by good friends is good for you. Trust God enough, in his all-knowing and unfailing love for you, to let him make his will for you clear in all three ways (height, width, and *depth*) before trying to move toward marriage.

The Questions You Ask

Pursue clarity and postpone intimacy. What does that look like practically? One test for whether you are pursuing clarity or intimacy is to study the questions you and your boyfriend or girlfriend ask in dating. We ask different questions when we're pursuing clarity more than intimacy.

- How far can we go?
- How late should we hang out?
- What kind of touching is allowed?
- Is he Christian *enough* for me to date him?

Versus:

- Does he love Jesus more than he loves me?
- Does she follow through on her promises?
- Do I see him showing self-control, or compromising to get what he wants?
- Is she willing to lovingly tell me when I'm wrong?

Healthy relationships may still need to ask questions in the first set, but they'll be way down the list. When we're after intimacy without clarity, we ask the first set and often overlook or minimize the second. But when we're pursuing clarity, we'll start asking new questions. Here are some examples of questions you and your boyfriend or girlfriend could ask in your pursuit of clarity:

- What new things have you learned about each other lately?
- How have you each grown in your relationship with Jesus since you started dating?
- Are you both committed to abstaining from sexual immorality?
- What flags, if any, have others raised about your relationship?
- What things are keeping the two of you from getting married?
- Are you each being driven by your own desires or by God's desires for you?
- In what ways is your relationship different from relationships in the world?

Questions like these uncover what we really want in dating and where we're likely to leave Jesus behind. They're the bumpers that keep us out of the gutter, guarding us from impatience and impurity. But they're also instruments of true love—the well-made parts that keep our car on the highway to marriage. They keep us focused on where we are headed and what really matters.

13

Sexual Freedom and Purity

I was not a virgin on my wedding day. Most people probably assumed I was. On paper I probably should have been. I grew up in a solid, Bible-believing, grace-filled Christian home, with a mom and a dad who loved me and were there for me in every way. They taught me to trust in and follow Jesus, to discern right from wrong, to exercise patience and self-control. I had great Christian friends, brothers in Christ who were walking alongside me, encouraging me, trying to hold me accountable, and pointing me to Jesus and to the cross. I lived the formula for sexual purity. But I still had sex before I graduated high school. No one knew for more than two years, no one except me, the girl whom I didn't guard or protect, and God.

I'll never forget the day my friend lovingly confronted me, uncovered the selfish darkness of my sin, and helped me begin to walk into forgiveness and freedom. The next several years were a mixture of victory and defeat in the battle for purity, sometimes fighting well and loving the girls I dated and other times failing to obey my Savior and to honor my sisters in Christ. I hate my sexual past, and I regret it all the time in marriage. I wish I could retrace every adrenaline-filled step I took into romance and intimacy and heal every wound I inflicted. I wish I had made Jesus look real, trustworthy, and satisfying in all my dating. I wish I could go back and save myself for Faye. I wish I could give her the priceless, awe-inspiring gift she gave me. I wish I could start all over again.

But strangely and beautifully, Faye would say she wouldn't trade anything about my past. It probably hurt her more than she's ever been hurt, but we believe we've seen and experienced Jesus walking together on *this* road more than we would have seen or experienced him on any other one. The gospel is *that* strange, *that* beautiful, *that* powerful. This chapter is a rallying cry to sexual selflessness, generosity, and patience. Whether you've never experimented sexually or have given yourself and your body away more times than you can count, you really can begin loving your future spouse and enjoying God's grace in sexual purity today.

Selfless Generosity

My favorite text in the Bible about sex isn't even about sex (and there are plenty about sex). Paul writes:

> If there is any encouragement in Christ, any comfort from love, any participation in the Spirit, any affection and sympathy, complete my joy by being of the same mind, having the same love, being in full accord and of one mind. Do nothing from selfish ambition or conceit, but in humility count others more significant than yourselves. Let each of you look not only to his own interests, but also to the interests of others. (Phil. 2:1–4)

Sex was meant to be selfless, to be a gift we give to our husband or wife, and to him or her alone. Paul writes, "The husband should give to his wife her conjugal rights, and likewise the wife to her husband" (1 Cor. 7:3). A husband *gives* sex to his wife, and a wife *gives* sex to her husband. Both looking *not* only to his or her own interests, but to the other's. Neither ever taking. Even though Paul mentions their rights, he doesn't tell them to demand anything. He's encouraging selfless sexual generosity—specifically and only between a husband and a wife—going to bed to please the other, not themselves. When sex is about selflessness and not self-gratification, we do what's best for the one we are dating and for our future spouse—even when that means rejecting our boyfriend's or girlfriend's premature desires for sexual intimacy. We're not enslaved by *our* desires anymore but freed from ourselves to serve one another in love.

Is that the way you think about sex? If you grew up watching cable television and mainstream movies, probably not. The lesson we hear and see in the world is that sex *is* fun and even valuable but selfish and fleeting. The sexy, tantalizing "love" of Hollywood mixes seduction, scandal, and passion. It suggests that the *best* love is found in forbidden love and with as many lovers as possible. Get yours—you "need" it, and you deserve it—but don't trust anyone. And don't be surprised if he leaves after he gets what he wants. Just move on.

The media says men have uncontrollable sexual cravings that have to be satisfied somewhere. Women are either helpless objects of their desires or wield their sexuality as an instrument of power and influence over men. The default sex education we receive in our world will produce only fallen, selfish ideas about sex, and false ideas produce bad decisions, and bad decisions produce bad habits, and bad habits breed shame, guilt, and hopelessness. *Sex* doesn't breed those things. Do you know that? Sex, as God designed it and gifted it to us to enjoy in marriage, breeds *life*, hope, and love for Jesus. Counterfeit sex—distorted sex, plagiarized sex, self-gratifying sex—steals the life and pleasure it was meant to give.

As Paul continues in Philippians 2, we see that the gospel presents a different picture for our lives, even our sex lives:

Have this mind among yourselves, which is yours in Christ Jesus, who, though he was in the form of God, did not count equality with God a thing to be grasped, but emptied himself, by taking the form of a servant, being born in the likeness of men. And being found in human form, he humbled himself by becoming obedient to the point of death, even death on a cross. (Phil. 2:5–8)

What if we loved our boyfriend or girlfriend (and future husband or wife) like that? When Paul was trying to describe Christian love, he drew a cross. When we're asking questions about how to date and where to draw the lines sexually, we should draw a cross. The cross was the highest act and expression of love the world has ever known, and it's the mold for our relationships and for our pursuit of sexual purity. If our love for one another looks selfish—if it takes rather than gives—it simply isn't love. But if we aim to love each other like Christ loved us on the cross, we'll avoid a lot of the sexual immorality, confusion, and heartache that are so common in dating. We'll love each other enough to say no. What if our love was so *strong* that it freed us from selfishly indulging now or taking anything from one another too soon? True love—the purest, fullest, most pleasing love—was designed by God for our good and then displayed by God at the cross. That's the love we need in marriage—sexual selflessness, generosity, and patience—so that's the kind of love we should be searching and waiting for in dating.

Sex Is Always War

We need to see that sex is a precious gift given to us by a creative and generous God. "'Therefore a man shall leave his father and mother and hold fast to his wife, and the two shall become one flesh.' This mystery is profound, and I am saying that it refers to Christ and the church" (Eph. 5:31–32). Sex—the two becoming *one* in marriage—was given to us to tell us something of the love, intimacy,

151

and trust we experience with God through Christ. Our relationship with God is not sexual, but sex in marriage—as the deepest, most vulnerable, most sacred act two people can enjoy together in this life—is a stunning picture of the height, length, width, and depth of God's love for us. It's a gift. Tim Keller says, "The Christian teaching is that sex is primarily a way to know God, and, if you use it for those things *rather* than for your own personal satisfaction, it will lead to greater fulfillment than you can imagine."[10]

But if we only ever think of it as a gift to us, we'll be prone to take it for granted or open it too soon. We also need to see that sex is war—not a battle of the sexes, but a war between good and evil. Paul writes:

> *Because of the temptation to sexual immorality*, each man should have his own wife and each woman her own husband. . . . Do not deprive one another, except perhaps by agreement for a limited time, that you may devote yourselves to prayer; but then come together again, *so that Satan may not tempt you* because of your lack of self-control. (1 Cor. 7:2–5)

One good reason we get married is to reject Satan's lies about sexual immorality and to satisfy our desires for sex and intimacy in healthy, Christ-exalting ways. It's one good reason to get married, and it's a good reason to keep having sex after we're married. Sex within marriage is an awesome act of spiritual war. Everything else—any sexual activity outside of the promises of marriage—is fighting for the other team. Satan has stolen sex and distorted it into something hideous and dangerous. The sex Satan sells is a counterfeit—a melting wax statue of the real thing. Instead of communicating the beauty and glory of God, it demonstrates the dangers of opposing him and corrupting his good gifts. Sex that rejects God rejects its *own* goodness. It misses the true point and pleasure of sex entirely.

Satan makes sexual sin look fun and harmless. In a society that downplays the evil of evil, and even glamorizes it, we need to be regularly reminded of the danger of sin. Like a child who discovers a needle on the street and thinks it's a toy, we can be dangerously naïve about the seriousness of sexual immorality. Sin is a needle that indulges deadly addictions and murders its victims. It is not the toy it pretends to be. It pierces quietly and deeply to the most vulnerable and longest-lasting parts of us. In whatever package—however romantic, exciting, and culturally accepted—it is not safe. Sin promises to please, but subtly and destructively wounds. "The sorrows of those who run after another god shall multiply" (Ps. 16:4). If you're honest, you don't really need to be persuaded of this. Anyone who has experimented with sin has known her to be a dishonest and unfaithful mistress. Sin presents itself—often persuasively—as fulfilling, reliable, and enduring. Instead of quenching the craving in our souls, though, it intensifies it. It doesn't satisfy our hunger; it only breeds it. Sin promises to produce happiness, but it only creates and multiplies pain, sadness, regret, and shame.

Sin that looks and feels like pleasure is only a poor shadow of something much more intense and satisfying. "I have set the LORD always before me; because he is at my right hand, I shall not be shaken. Therefore my heart is glad, and my whole being rejoices. . . . In your presence there is fullness of joy, at your right hand are pleasures forevermore" (Ps. 16:8–11). There's no question: when we indulge the desires of our flesh in a relationship, we will feel some kind of sensation and even pleasure. Sin wouldn't have any power over us if we didn't. The promise we're forgetting or rejecting, though, is that the thimble of pleasure we receive in sin is short and pathetic compared with the ocean of pleasure we will have in God's presence.

Costly Grace and Cheap Sex

Sexual selflessness, generosity, and patience look like Jesus's love for us on the cross, and they also look *to* that love and sacrifice as their driving hope and incentive. Paul writes, "Flee from sexual immorality. . . . Or do you not know that your body is a temple of the Holy Spirit within you, whom you have from God? You are not your own, for you were bought with a price. So glorify God in your body" (1 Cor. 6:18–20).

When you begin to feel overwhelmed with temptation and the desires are raging inside you, remember that you were bought with a price, paid for in full with blood. Sadly, many of us take the purchase of grace at infinite cost, and foolishly and suicidally justify more sin. We assume Jesus will just forgive us, again. But the cross—those two grace-charged beams of murderous wood—call us to do exactly the opposite. God spent the precious, sinless blood of his one and only Son not just to forgive our sin, but to keep us from it. He wanted us to see the thorns in his head, the open flesh in his back, and the nails in his wrists, and to run like crazy away from sin. When we begin to realize that we will never be able to grasp the fullness of the love God revealed in Jesus's wounds, in his agony, in his last breath, we will dread doing anything to make that price look cheap. And our sexual immorality makes the cross look cheap, like a clearance-rack redemption.

But when we choose to pursue purity and postpone intimacy, Jesus's sacrifice looks costly, like our most expensive and prized possession. When we do not push boundaries, we announce the priceless weight of every one of his wounds. When we keep our clothes on and our hands from wandering, we celebrate the immeasurable mercy he carried on a back destroyed with lashes. When we wait in dating, we declare again that he really is risen from the dead and reigning in heaven. Our sexual purity will either make the cross look real and valuable, or it won't.

With our eyes happily fixed on Jesus, the once-for-all sacrifice for our sins, he will increasingly be honored in our bodies, whether in singleness or in marriage. Looking to the cross and all Jesus paid to make us his own, we trust God for the grace and courage to resist our impulses to dishonor him and to disgrace the cross and instead to wield our God-given and grace-filled bodies to honor him, to glorify him, and to help others see the beauty of his strength, wisdom, love, and sufficiency. With every second we deny selfish sexual desires, we say that we trust him more than we trust ourselves, and we say that he is more than enough for us.

Date Like You Know God

At its simplest, we should date as people who know God. Paul says, "This is the will of God, your sanctification: that you abstain from sexual immorality; that each one of you know how to control his own body in holiness and honor, not in the passion of lust like the Gentiles *who do not know God*" (1 Thess. 4:3–5). The Gentiles—people in the world and not in Christ—are involved in all kinds of sexual nonsense, and that makes sense, because they don't know God. We should expect them to go too far and too fast—to fool around with the random person at the party or to sleep with their third or fourth person in a month or to move in with their boyfriend. If God is out of the picture, sex can be as good a god as any. It will still fail them forever, but that doesn't bother them, because they don't believe in Jesus or sin, heaven or hell. They believe in *now*, in living it up here on earth as much as possible and for as long as possible.

But we know better. We know that sin, death, and hell are as real as the roof over our heads, last month's cell phone bill, and the Grand Canyon. They're not ideas flying around in our philosophy class. They're realities hanging over every inch of our lives, including our sex lives. We live every moment in the shadow of a real creator and a real judge, one who knows our every thought and move. We know that we deserve less than nothing because of our sin, that we've earned conscious, relentless, inescapable destruction for ourselves, and that "everyone who is sexually immoral or impure . . . has *no* inheritance in the kingdom of Christ and God" (Eph. 5:5). And we know that Christ came to die—the crown of thorns, the whip filled with rocks, the nails in his hands and feet, the terrifying wrath of God—for *our* sin and to rescue us out of sin.

God made each of us and invented sex; why would we act like we know better than he? God warns us that sexual immorality leads only to pain, shame, slavery, and ultimately judgment; why would we risk so much for a little pleasure now? God bought our forgiveness, freedom, and purity with the blood of his own Son— an infinite cost; why would we heave more sin on his shoulders and drive the nails even deeper? God waits with open arms to welcome us into a never-ending adventure of peace and happiness with him; why would we trade it away for a few seconds of satisfaction? Sadly, some of us still do. Temptation overwhelms us in moments of weakness. But Paul is saying that what we already know about God is enough to keep us from sexual sin. To know God—his sovereign power, his surprising mercy, his sacrificial love, his satisfying friendship—is to hold the keys to sexual purity, even in a sex-crazed society. As we set our eyes and hearts above, "the love of Christ controls us" (2 Cor. 5:14), and more and more, we "know how to control [our] own body in holiness and honor, not in the passion of lust" (1 Thess. 4:4–5). We put on sexual selflessness, generosity, and patience.

Sexual Failure

For some of you, all of this has been a deepening of what you've already pursued and practiced. Others of you have had a hard time reading this chapter because of sinful choices you've made. And you know now, more than ever before, that you were so wrong. That's my story. These have been the most devastating pages to write. I couldn't give Faye the gift of a lifetime of sexual patience and purity. Instead of anticipating enjoying sex for the first time together, I had to confess I had already been there. That she wouldn't be my first.

I'll never forget where we were the day I told Faye about my past. We started dating May 1, and on May 2 almost exactly one year later, we had the hardest conversation we've probably ever had. I could walk you to the place on the beach where I struggled for more than thirty minutes to get our umbrella to stand upright in the wind. Eventually, I was forced to surrender and rest it on the ground. I remember her Ironman tank top. I'll remember May 2, in part, because of the brokenness I carried into it. I'm not sure the weight of all my sin has ever felt so heavy. I loved her. And I wanted her to love me and marry me. But she hadn't seen all of me yet, and I didn't know how she would respond to all of this. I knew she had saved herself for her husband. I was ready for her to tell me it was over.

The main reason May 2 will be stamped on my memory, though, was her response to my past. My record of sins fell heavily on her. She was sad, even heartbroken. But God. When she describes it today, she says a wave of grace fell on her in those moments like never before. She sensed God's unexpected and undeniable nearness to her. She listened. She grieved. And then she simply and lovingly expressed her unshakeable hope *in* Jesus *for* me. The gospel had been real to me for a long time, but never this real. Her heart and her words enabled new senses. It was as if I had been looking at an ocean all my life, enjoying all the colors of blue, loving the rhythms of peace and violence, occasionally spotting a sailboat or even a dolphin. And then suddenly I could *smell* the fresh seawater, and *taste* the salt in the air, and *hear* the waves crashing and the seagulls flying overhead, and I could *feel* the sand, with the water splashing over my feet. I had known the gospel, had believed the gospel, and even *loved* the gospel. But now I was immersed in it, neck-deep and wading deeper with my best friend and future bride.

If you have failed sexually (or sinned in any other way), God can still wash you in grace like that, regardless of how your boyfriend, or girlfriend, responds to your past. Grace doesn't undo the sins we've committed, but it redeems them and makes them work for our good. It never overlooks or okays sexual sin (Rom. 6:1–2). But it will cover every forgiven sin and cast it as far as the east is from the west, into the very deepest, most hidden and forgotten parts of the sea (Mic. 7:19). Your past sexual sin cannot overcome the sovereign love displayed for you at the cross, and it cannot keep you from pure, blameless, and everlasting joy. That is, if you will believe in the one who took on your sin for you, even your sexual sin, and if you repent and pursue his purity by his grace in his strength.

14

Acts of War in Love

My wife and I love the beach. She lived near a dozen beautiful beaches outside of Los Angeles until I ripped her away to snowy Minnesota. We have water in Minneapolis; it's just frozen half the year. Part of enjoying the beach, at least in California, is enjoying the sunshine. We have weather like theirs here too—blue skies, burning sun, light breeze—at least for two or three weeks every year. More than half of enjoying the beach, though, is being able to stand *that* close to something *that* big. Something happens deep inside of us when we let the water splash over our feet and stare out over endless waves that extend far beyond where our imagination can run. It's estimated that the Pacific Ocean holds 187 *quintillion* gallons (eighteen zeroes) of water. Scientists have discovered at least one place in the ocean that's almost *seven miles* deep. And we can safely play there in its wake at Newport Beach, wading carelessly into seemingly infinite power and mystery.

How is something that big that safe for us? It is safe because God holds it back with a word. The Lord says to Job,

> Who shut in the sea with doors
>   when it burst out from the womb,

> when I made clouds its garment
>   and thick darkness its swaddling band,
> and prescribed limits for it
>   and set bars and doors,
> and said, "Thus far shall you come, and no farther,
>   and here shall your proud waves be stayed"?
>   (Job 38:8–11)

He created something as massive and powerful as the ocean to show us a little picture of his power. He wanted to give us categories for *his* bigness and majesty. And then he drew a line in the sand and told the waves they could go no farther. "He established the fountains of the deep, when he assigned to the sea its limit, so that the waters might not transgress his command, when he marked out the foundations of the earth" (Prov. 8:28–29). He set a boundary to show us that the waves are his, to tell us that he is sovereign, creative, and wise—and that he can be trusted.

God does the same kind of work in marriage and dating. As we walk up to the edge of marriage, we draw close to something so much bigger than ourselves. There's a power and a mystery in such love. It's a vibrant picture of the love God has shown us in sending his Son, a love wider and deeper than the Pacific Ocean. God designed love in marriage, like gallons and gallons of ocean, to show us how unsearchable *his* love is for us. We could never contain it or know it completely. And because love within a covenant is so large, so intense, so captivating, he established a boundary, a shoreline. He drew a line in the sand for our safety and to secure our greatest happiness in marriage.

Setting good boundaries in dating will rest on recognizing and even appreciating God's one massive boundary. Any woman who is not your wife is not your wife. Any man who is not your husband is not your husband. "Each man should have his own wife and each woman her own husband" (1 Cor. 7:2). No almost-husbands, no kind-of-wives, no probably-one-day marriages. God intended for *one* man to be joined with *one* woman in the promises of marriage, and he intended for us to enjoy marital intimacy and pleasure, especially sexual intimacy and pleasure, only in the context of those promises. Sex is reserved for the ocean deeps of marriage, not the safe wading depth of dating.

But Satan is still telling the same lies he was telling in the garden when he convinced Adam and Eve to eat the fruit. God said to Adam, "You may surely eat of every tree of the garden, but of the tree of the knowledge of good and evil you shall not eat, for in the day that you eat of it you shall surely die" (Gen. 2:16–17). You may eat of *every* tree but one. Satan took the infinite creativity and generosity of the Father and made him sound stingy. "He said to the woman, 'Did God actually say, "You shall not eat of any tree in the garden"?'" (Gen. 3:1). Do you hear the manipulation and deception—making freedom look like slavery? Why did God tell them not to eat from the one tree? "For in the day that you eat of it you shall surely *die*." He wasn't trying to deprive them. He was trying to *save* them. Satan took the infinite wisdom and love of the Father and made him sound overprotective. "The serpent said to the woman, 'You will not surely die'" (Gen. 3:4). He made suicide seem harmless. And he still tells the same lies in dating today. He takes the wisdom and love in good boundaries and makes them look stingy, overprotective, and unnecessary.

Redefining Boundaries

What are we really after in dating (or in all of life)? What are we trying to secure or enjoy in this relationship? If the honest answer is affection and intimacy, no number of boundaries can guard us completely. We can put up all the fences we want, but the brokenness hides inside of us (and all our fences), and it waits to strike when we're at our weakest and most vulnerable. If we're able to answer that we're after more of Jesus in dating and in marriage, the boundaries that once looked so stale, boring, and old-fashioned suddenly become our best friends in the fight. They're the courageous, faith-filled steps we take to find more of Jesus together. They're the battles we win together against all of Satan's worst attacks.

We get so defensive about dating—always on guard *against* evil, always fighting *against* temptation. But what if the boundaries we keep were really meant to help us fight *for* something? What if, instead of fence building, they were acts of war in love? Boundaries are hard to keep, at least in part, because Satan convinces us we're only sacrificing and never gaining, that we're holed up in this dark, cold, damp cave called "Christian dating." He makes Christian dating sound like slavery. Christ came to us not to enslave us, though, but to liberate us. "For freedom Christ has set us free" (Gal. 5:1). A life in Christ is a life of freedom. There *is* sacrifice in this relationship, but it's not worth comparing with our reward. There *are* patience and self-control, but they don't quench love. They nourish and strengthen the kind of love we're really longing for. The boundaries—these spiritual acts of war—don't steal anything from us. They're the tracks on which we run the fastest and freest with Jesus (and each other). Every act of obedience, in life and in dating, is a free act of defiance in the face of Satan's schemes and lies. We're not just *guarding* ourselves from him, but we're *seizing* territory back from him.

Three Acts of War in Love

We're going to look at three sets of boundaries we need in dating, three spiritual acts of war in relationships. Boundaries like these are essential if we want to date differently from the world and in line with the gospel.

1. Cultivate independence from one another.

We all want to start with physical boundaries—touching, kissing, and beyond—but those are not the first dangers we face on the road of any relationship. We're quick to feel guilty about breaking physical boundaries, but our feelings are really the first battlefield, and some of the easiest ground we give up. While we're focused on how far is too far physically, our hearts really make up the couple of inches that matter most to God. Will we let our imagination and emotions run far out ahead of where the relationship really is, or will we guard our heart? Will we bind ourselves emotionally or spiritually to someone in a way we should only lean on a spouse? Emotions feel so natural and innocent. How could they be wrong?

"The heart is deceitful above all things, and desperately sick" (Jer. 17:9), especially when it is lovesick. The hard reality about our heart reality is that we simply cannot trust our feelings—even after we're saved. Emotional boundaries *are* less objective, by nature, because they are the lines we draw in our own hearts. Are my feelings and emotions in line with the realities of the relationship and with the gospel? Or am I allowing my emotions to run ahead and take control? In some ways, emotional and spiritual boundaries take even more effort and discipline because they aren't as tangible and concrete as touching.

Lean in to your closest friends and be as honest as possible. Talk through where your heart really is—what you are treasuring most, what you are expecting from your dating relationship, and how willing you are to compromise. Good friends will be able to tell if the one you are dating has drawn you closer to Christ or away. And they will be able to tell if you're depending on your boyfriend or girlfriend in unhealthy ways. Until we are married, we should develop and maintain a healthy independence from our significant other and prepare ourselves for the possibility that God's plans may be different from our own. Without a ring on our finger, we simply do not know what God will do with this relationship. "Keep your heart with all vigilance, for from it flow the springs of life" (Prov. 4:23). Guard your body *and* your heart.

2. *Take time to talk about talking.*

Most of you have never thought of setting conversational boundaries. I wasn't ready when a girlfriend's dad asked in the first couple months of our relationship, "Have you mentioned marriage yet?" *Long awkward pause.* "Um, yeah . . . I think we did talk about it once."

"I don't think that was appropriate for you to talk about, and I expect you to care for her better than that."

I was totally caught off guard. I had never even thought of certain topics of conversation as inappropriate or dangerous. If dating is supposed to be the pursuit of marriage, don't we have to talk about marriage?

Yes, we do, but carefully, and at the right times. For some of us, talking about marriage can be as intimate as making out, or even more. Within marriage, trust isn't meant only for the bedroom but for all of life. We weren't meant to build a blueprint for life with three or four almost-spouses. It's fun and exciting to talk about what time of year we might get married or how many kids we might have or where we might vacation or what kind of ministry we might take on together, but it can be as spiritually dangerous as sexual immorality. You'll have to have certain conversations eventually, but don't rush into them, and when you do have them, have them with caution and self-control. You will be able to safely enjoy dreaming together without a hint of guilt or danger, for years and years, *if* you get married.

There are at least two categories to think about when it comes to conversations with your boyfriend or girlfriend. First, monitor how much you talk and how much time you spend together. If we're serious about guarding our hearts and minds, developing healthy independence, and anchoring our hope and joy in Jesus more than in each other, we'll be careful with how much time we're focused on one another. It may feel ridiculous and unnecessary to resist the impulse to talk all the time—you're both curious and excited and ready to hang out—but it will serve you so well in the future, whether you get married or not. Faye and I were long-distance, so we talked once a week (or so) initially, and after that a couple times a week. After six months or so, we started talking most days. We never got in a habit of talking for hours every night. We've never regretted that in marriage, and we've had every opportunity to make up for any lost time. I don't say that to try to limit you but to give you categories for deliberate self-control and patience. You'll have to talk about what seems healthy and appropriate for you, and ask friends and family if they agree. It won't happen by accident, so don't be afraid to initiate the conversation about your conversations.

Second, think about *what* you talk about when you do talk. Limiting your time will focus your conversations; at least it did for us. Trading two or three or four hours for forty minutes meant we were more intentional with what we talked about. You don't have to figure out your whole future together by the third date. You don't have to talk about your relationship every time you talk, or even half the time. You don't need to remind each other every fifteen minutes why you like each other. You really don't need to talk much about marriage until it's reasonable that you might actually get engaged and married soon. Conversations can become places we compromise without feeling like we're compromising. We indulge desires for intimacy without touching. Have a conversation about how often you should check in about your relationship. Talk about a good timeline to talk about marriage. Determine the relationship every now and then, and communicate your feelings and intentions clearly, but spend significantly more time talking about what God is teaching each of you, how you're growing in your faith, and where you're spending your energy and gifts for the sake of others.

3. Value trusting each other more than touching each other.
Several years ago I asked one of my pastors about physical boundaries in dating. He said, "I've done more than a hundred weddings

over the last twenty-five years and premarital counseling for almost all of those couples. Not one of them *ever* regretted a boundary they set in dating, and almost every one wished they had set more." He didn't draw specific lines for me that day, but he didn't have to. He just confidently assured me that I would never regret something we didn't do in dating but we'd probably regret the things we didn't wait to do—*even* if we ended up getting married. He testified to all the couples who had sat in premarital counseling, about to get married, wishing they hadn't touched *each other* so much already, wishing they could enjoy all those things together for the first time in marriage.

Why is that? Because God means for us to have clarity, and *then* intimacy. Marriage, *and then* sexual activity. That means we should start valuing *trusting* each other more than *touching* each other. Don't just *avoid* sexual immorality, but *pursue* patience, self-control, and trust. Think of everything you don't do together now as something you *are* doing together to maximize your happiness and freedom in marriage.

Touching almost always leads to more touching, and it makes touching in dating hazardous, like the powerful undertow in the Pacific Ocean. If you've ever waded out far enough into any ocean, you've felt the waves start to take over. From the first time you even hug or hold hands, you'll feel a pull to touch more—more often and more intimately. You swim out a little further, thinking you can handle it, that you're in control and can calmly paddle back at any time. And then suddenly you're gasping for air and desperately flailing against the current. You're crossing boundaries you didn't mean to cross, and you don't know how to stop. Instead of surrendering and wading, we should be fighting and waiting.

I asked Faye if I could hold her hand after four months of dating. Fifteen months later, we kissed for the first time on a pier at Newport Beach, moments after she agreed to marry me. We dated very happily for nineteen months without kissing. I don't offer our experience as any kind of gold standard, but I can tell you we do not regret not touching more in dating. In fact, our sense is that God has rewarded every ounce of patience and self-control with deeper enjoyment of each other in marriage.

While Faye and I were dating, someone asked me one of the most helpful and penetrating questions related to physical boundaries: "Will you feel the need to apologize to her future spouse?" If the two of you do not get married (and that's as likely as any outcome at this point), and you saw your girlfriend with her future spouse one day, would you be proud of how you treated her—what you said, how far things went, the boundaries you kept or crossed, the way you touched her—or would you be ashamed and feel the need to apologize? Honest answers to that question will uncover a lot of wrong ideas, desires, and behaviors in dating. How sweet would it be if that future spouse could look you in the eyes, knowing everything about your relationship with his now-spouse, and *thank* you for loving his wife (and Jesus) enough *not* to take advantage of her or push the boundaries physically. Date her, in every area of dating, so that you could freely and joyfully stand before God and her future spouse one day without any shade of regret or shame.

Speak Up and Take the Lead

Husbands are called to lead and serve their wives (Eph. 5:23). Boyfriends are likewise (not in the same way) called to lead and serve their girlfriends in dating—to be the selfless initiator and protector. Boyfriends are not husbands, and they should not act like husbands. But they should act like men. Men in the world are known for pushing the boundaries. What if men in the church were known instead for championing the boundaries—for being outspoken about the dangers of sin, for pushing pause when temptations rise, for pursuing women with stunning purity—in summary, for treating women like Jesus treats us (Eph. 5:25–27)?

What does that kind of selfless leadership look like in dating? It begins with communication (another major weakness among most men). Men, declare your intentions clearly, set the pace, and communicate progress. Let's be the ones to initiate the hard conversations about boundaries and purity. It may not feel comfortable or romantic in the moment, but she will adore you for it down the road (and hopefully even now). Don't hold a press conference to announce the state of the relationship on every date—a temptation on the other side—but consistently communicate where this relationship is headed and how you think things are going. When everyone else is "just talking" or hooking up randomly, your girlfriend should never wonder what you are thinking, wanting, or feeling about the relationship, at least not about anything significant. Ambiguity is a weapon of manipulation in dating, not a way to move toward marriage. Let's be bold enough *not* to push the boundaries and brave enough to bring up the boundaries when temptations come. Don't wait for her to say no. Love her enough to never make her draw the line.

But, women, this is not a get-out-of-jail-free card for you when it comes to boundaries. Your boyfriend *should* take responsibility and protect you. If he doesn't, you should question whether he's ready to pursue marriage and to love you as his wife. He may be fun, charming, and physically attractive, but will he lay down his own interests and desires for your sake? If your boyfriend is not willing or able to enforce the boundaries you've set, you should be. The joy and hope you've found in Jesus should free you to quickly and emphatically say no when necessary. If you're uncomfortable, tell him immediately. If you have questions—any question—about the boundaries or his behavior or the status of your relationship, ask him. You may be afraid to lose him because you drew the line, confronted him, or asked an "awkward" question.

But if he's not ready to be honest with you and actively pursue purity, you really should be more afraid of *not* losing him. You do not need him, or this relationship, and certainly not any shame or regret from crossing boundaries. Tell him no, and if he resists, break up with him.

Satan wants us to believe life and joy are on the far side of these boundaries—in wading out into the overpowering ocean of our desires, risking everything to go just a little farther out—but those who have tasted real life and joy know the safety and pleasure of waiting inside the shoreline God has established for us in dating.

15

The Third Wheel We All Need

We all know we don't know enough to live. We know we need other people's knowledge and experience to get by. Don't believe me? Just look at your search history. We really know, more than anyone in history, just how much we do not know. Fortunately, we don't have to know everything. We live in an age when we literally never have to wait for an answer. If it can be known, we know it in seconds, probably less. Google, living and active, lies at our disposal on every device we own. No one ever has to not know again.

In fact, we're now much more likely to look online for help than to ask someone we know. Why is that? Well, in part because Google knows so much more than any of our friends (any of my friends, anyway). But we also run to Google because Google is a low-commitment, hands-free counselor and friend—always available whenever we need it and never asking us for anything. The red, yellow, blue, and green god at our fingertips is visible, controllable, instant, and seemingly omniscient, at least omniscient enough for us. It's a never-ending buffet of opinions and advice that has something to say about everything and yet lets us choose the answer we want, especially in dating.

- How far should we go physically before marriage?
- How soon should I start dating after a breakup?
- What things should I be looking for in a guy?
- What are girls looking for in a guy?
- Should couples live together before getting married?

We won't have trouble finding an answer (or a thousand answers) to any of our questions in relationships. The scary reality is that we can find an answer somewhere online to justify what we want to do—right or wrong, safe or unsafe, wise or unwise. The advice we choose might be from a book by a doctor, or a blog post by a teenager, or just something we found on Pinterest. It really doesn't matter who's offering the advice as long as it confirms what we thought or wanted in the first place. We think we're leaning on others as we wade into all the material online, but we're often just surrendering to our own cravings and ignorance. We leave the safety of the doctor's office and choose the freedom and ease of the gas station convenience store. Instead of getting the qualified perspective and direction we desperately need from people around us, we walk away eating our favorite candy bar for dinner, again, and wash it down with some Dr. Pepper.

Real friendship, with real life-on-life accountability, may not offer the same amount of information or advice, and you may not always like what it has to say, but it will bring one new critical dimension to your dating relationships: it knows *you*. Google may know lots of things about you, but it will never know you, and it will never use what it does know in love for you. It doesn't want to make you a better person or help you make better decisions in dating. Google wants us to keep clicking, not growing. Google gives us what we want, not what we need. We all need a third wheel—in life and in dating—people who truly know us and love us, and who want what's best for us, even if it's not what we want in the moment.

The Burdens We Bear Alone

The first Bible verse I can remember memorizing is Galatians 6:2: "Bear one another's burdens, and so fulfill the law of Christ." I memorized those eleven words with a half dozen other guys my freshman year in high school. Our Young Life leader gave us that verse to teach us that we needed one another as we followed Jesus. Our faith was our own, and our relationship with Jesus was our own, but we were never meant to walk alone. We had to learn to bear others' burdens and, maybe more difficult, to be willing to let others help us carry ours.

Even today, though, I'm tempted to define *burdens* here as once-in-a-while, especially serious needs. "If you ever need anything, you know I'll be there for you." It's a safeguard we put in place for unexpected or overwhelming crises; for example, a death in the family, an unexpected financial need, a serious illness, or a job loss. But we don't really expect to need one another, at least not often. That kind of individuality and independence is more American than Christian. When Paul told us to carry each other's burdens, he was talking mainly about our hearts, about the things that happen *inside* of us, not outside. And the burdens he had in mind were not extraordinary, but ordinary. He was tying us together not mainly to preserve one another's sanity and comfort in the midst of life's most intense trials but to help us be faithful to Jesus in the midst of life's more mundane frustrations and temptations.

How do I know that? The verses immediately before Galatians 6:2 are not about sickness, poverty, or even persecution—not about the things we usually think about as burdens. No, Paul talks about walking by the Spirit—trading the world's path to comfort and pleasure for the path of life. "I say, walk by the Spirit, and you will not gratify the desires of the flesh" (Gal. 5:16). He's not trying to save us from discomfort or inconvenience but from sin—from "sexual immorality, impurity, sensuality, idolatry, sorcery, enmity, strife, jealousy, fits of anger, rivalries, dissensions, divisions, envy, drunkenness, orgies, and things like these" (Gal. 5:19–21). He's not mainly thinking about fulfilling our *physical* needs, but our spiritual ones—"love, joy, peace, patience, kindness, goodness, faithfulness, gentleness, self-control" (Gal. 5:22–23). He ends chapter 5 by saying, "If we live by the Spirit, let us also keep in step with the Spirit" (v. 25). And then he begins chapter 6 with bearing one another's burdens, the burdens of living passionately and faithfully, step by step, for Jesus.

Truly Known and Deeply Loved

This chapter is a call to accountability in dating—to bearing each other's burdens in the pursuit of marriage. Maybe that term—*accountability*—has dried out and gone stale in your life. To be accountable is to be truly, deeply, consistently known by someone who cares enough to keep us from making mistakes or indulging in sin. The Bible warns us to weave all our desires, needs, and decisions deep into a fabric of family who love us and will help us follow Jesus. God has sent you—your faith, your gifts, and your experience—into other believers' lives for their good to encourage them: "We urge you, brothers, admonish the idle, *encourage the fainthearted*, help the weak, be patient with them all" (1 Thess. 5:14); to challenge and correct them: "Let the word of Christ dwell in you richly, teaching and admonishing one another in all wisdom" (Col. 3:16); and to build them up: "Therefore encourage one another and build one another up" (1 Thess. 5:11). And as inconvenient, unnecessary, unhelpful, and even unpleasant as it may feel at times, God has sent gifted, experienced, Christ-loving men and women into your life too, for *your* good. The God who sends these people into our lives knows what we need far better than we ever will.

The people willing to hold me accountable in dating have been my best friends. I've had lots of friends over the years, but the ones who have been willing to press in, ask harder questions, and offer unwanted (but wise) counsel are the friends I respect and prize the most. They stepped in when I was spending too much time with a girlfriend or started neglecting other important areas of my life. They raised a flag when a relationship seemed unhealthy. They knew where I had fallen before in sexual purity, and they weren't afraid to ask questions to protect me. They have relentlessly pointed me to Jesus—reminding me not to put my hope in any relationship, to pursue patience and purity, and to communicate and lead well. These guys didn't perfectly guard me from mistake or failure—no one can—but they played a massive role in helping me mature as a man, a boyfriend, and now as a husband. We all need courageous, persistent, and hopeful friends and counselors in the dangerous and murky waters of dating.

Four Sets of Eyes and Hearts
There are several different relationships in our lives that each play a unique role in our dating relationships: our church family, our parents, our friends, and the Lord. Together they offer four levels of accountability.

1. Avoid leaving your church family behind in dating.
We don't usually think of our church family as part of our pursuit of marriage. Many of us probably don't even want them to be involved. We tend to distance ourselves from others when we start to get serious about someone, focusing all our time and energy on our boyfriend or girlfriend. But God gives the primary and final responsibility for our accountability to the local church (Matt. 18:15–17). He means for the church to be the rough tread on the edge of the highway, making sure we stay awake and alert while driving in life, and in dating. If we don't build our church family into our routine and our relationships, we're likely to ride right off into a ditch. Most of the time, we don't stop and thank God for

those treads until we need them, but we're glad they're there if we start to fall asleep at the wheel. The church offers us that kind of structure, direction, and safety.

Churches are filled with different kinds of people—different ages; different careers, hobbies, and lifestyles; different ethnicities; different stages of life. Some of the best accountability will come from those who are nothing like us or our friends. We are always tempted to surround ourselves with people who think like us, live like us, and even look like us. And we gravitate to those with similar circumstances (college, singleness, business, marriage, children). The church folds us into a family with people who are nothing like us. That diversity is not a weekly trial to endure; it's an unbelievable gift and privilege. You don't have to stand up during the announcements and give the whole church an update on your relationship or print a weekly update in the bulletin. But lean on some people who are older and more mature than you. Let a few people you wouldn't hang out with on the weekends into your thinking and decision making in dating.

Some of you aren't members of a local church right now. In fact, for any number of reasons, you're not even attending a church. You might be putting off joining a church until you get married and start a family. The problem is, you need the church right now, and the church needs you. Paul says, "Now you are the body of Christ and individually members of it" (1 Cor. 12:27), and "God arranged the members in the body, each one of them, as he chose" (12:18). If we are believers in Jesus, we *are* a part of his body—a hand, a foot, an ear, a kidney. The question is whether we will be a healthy member, or a lame, dysfunctional, and useless one. Paul goes on, "God has so composed the body . . . that there may be no division in the body, but that the members may have the same care for one another. If one member suffers, all suffer together; if one member is honored, all rejoice together" (1 Cor. 12:24–26). When we leave the church behind, we rob the body of that kind of support and joy. And we sacrifice the same for ourselves. Be accountable to a local church: plug in, get to know and be known by a few people, seek out people different from you, and draw them into your dating life.

2. Lean into the love that made and raised you.

"Honor your father and mother" (Eph. 6:2; Ex. 20:12). It's so simple and yet so challenging. It seems old-fashioned and unnecessary today. Parents are a formality once we've made our decision in dating—unless, of course, we're committed to dating distinctly from the world and pursuing marriage in a way that tells others about Jesus. Including and honoring our parents in dating isn't popular, and it won't always be easy. Maybe we don't see eye to eye with our parents. Maybe our parents aren't believers. Maybe our parents are divorced and disagree with each other about what we should do. Maybe one or both aren't even interested in being involved in our relationship. We can't force them to care or cooperate, but we can honor them, and we can think of creative ways to encourage them to be involved and to solicit their input and advice. Even if you don't agree with them about your relationship (maybe *especially* if you disagree with them), lean in and listen well. If they're worried or frustrated, work as hard as you can to understand why. Our parents may be flat-out wrong, but most parents don't intentionally want to harm us or keep us from being happy. It's easy to give up quickly and check out. Let's shock everyone by loving our parents *more* intentionally and *more* joyfully when we disagree with them.

What about the girlfriend's father? As a trend, dads seem to be less and less involved in their daughter's dating. Wise boyfriends seek out their girlfriend's dad and try to learn as much as possible about how to care for her from the man who has been most responsible for caring for her. Too often, we've relegated dads to a last-minute interview before engagement, when God meant for them to be active, available agents of wisdom and safekeeping. And I don't mean policemen. Foolish dads relish the gun-bearing, tough-guy role. Wise dads relish the opportunity to develop a real, intentional, grace-and-truth relationship with the man who might be tasked with caring for their daughter for the rest of her life. What if a daughter's father took some responsibility not just in *vetting* a young man but in *investing* in him and preparing him to make much of Jesus in dating and marriage? And what if, as boyfriends, we were bold enough to initiate that kind of relationship and discipleship with her father?[11]

Some of you may have been reading and despairing. Unfortunately, physically or functionally, there are a lot of fatherless sons and daughters in the world and in the church. You might have lost your dad as a child. Disease, an accident, addiction, violence— there's no easy way to lose him. It hurts, and it keeps hurting. But our God is not only a God for the fathered. More than anyone in history, he loves the orphan, those abandoned biologically as well as those who've been left spiritually. And he has wonderfully provided men to father when fathers can't or won't. In your average, Bible-loving, evangelical church, there are very likely faithful, Jesus-following, older men who can help you walk through your relationship. They can love you and your girlfriend or boyfriend well and lead the two of you toward safety in your intimacy and clarity about the future.

3. Surround your relationship with real friends.

The next line of defense in dating are the friends who know us, our boyfriend or girlfriend, and our relationship best and love us and Jesus enough to hold us accountable. We don't need just friends. Everybody has friends. We need *real* friends who know us well enough and who are regularly and actively involved in our relationship.

By ourselves, we do not have all the perspective and wisdom

we need to honor Christ in dating. We may think we have everything figured out and under control, but the Bible says clearly we should never live (or date) like that. Proverbs warns us, "Without counsel plans fail, but with many advisers they succeed" (Prov. 15:22). And Hebrews says, "Take care, brothers, lest there be in any of you an evil, unbelieving heart, leading you to fall away from the living God. But exhort one another every day, as long as it is called 'today,' that none of you may be hardened by the deceitfulness of sin" (Heb. 3:12–13). Every day. Every season of life. Every relationship. We should be suspicious enough of our sinful hearts to get a second opinion. Even after God rescues us from our sin, pulls us out of the pit, and puts his Spirit inside us, we still battle remaining sin in our hearts, and we're outmatched on our own. We need friends in the fight to help us find where we are wrong or weak.

Do not wait for a friend to ask you how things are going. Seek out those few friends and share openly. Don't make them ask really good questions. Be prepared to admit your insecurities and inadequacies and to confess your failures. Confession is a means of grace, not of judgment. James says, "Therefore, confess your sins to one another and pray for one another, *that you may be healed*" (James 5:16). If you don't know what to ask a friend about his or her relationship, or if you're looking for questions to have others ask you, here are some important ones:

- What do the two of you talk about? What's a typical conversation like?
- How far have you gone physically, and in what situations do you experience the most temptation?
- What boundaries have the two of you put in place? Have you been able to keep those boundaries?
- What are you learning about him (or her)? Are you moving toward or away from clarity about marriage?

- How has your relationship affected your relationship with the Lord—prayer, Bible reading, involvement in the local church, and ministry to others?

4. *Examine yourself before the Lord.*

If we do not take our responsibility to God seriously, we'll never take our accountability to others seriously. The friendships we need most in this life are built on shared convictions: God *really* exists and knows absolutely everything about us. Sin *really* sends us to hell, apart from faith and repentance. Jesus *really* bled and suffocated on a cross to save us. We *really* are blind to some of the remaining sin still inside of us. Without such convictions, we're really just playing church in our accountability. All the conversations look safe, significant, and Christian, but we're not really trusting each other or Jesus to go to the places we need to go.

The accountability we need from others will always begin with us, with our own sense of accountability *to God.* "Examine *your-selves,* to see whether you are in the faith. Test yourselves" (2 Cor. 13:5). No one under heaven knows you more than you do, and no one under heaven has more at stake in your life and future than you do. That should make us more concerned than anyone with our own faith and faithfulness, with whether we prove ourselves to be genuine, fruit-bearing believers in Christ and his grace.

Right after Paul tells us to carry *each other's* burdens, he says, "*But let each one test his own work*, and then his reason to boast will be in himself alone and not in his neighbor. For each will have to bear his own load" (Gal. 6:3–5). What does that mean? Accountability is absolutely critical ("carry each other's burdens"), but we each stand alone on judgment day. No one else's faith or love for us or concern for our salvation will count for us then; only our own faith and the evidences of grace in our life. Therefore, in addition to our accountability to others, we each test our own work—attitudes, decisions, and behaviors. In our dating, are we walking "worthy of the gospel of Christ" (Phil. 1:27), or are we settling for a discount "Christian" relationship that looks an awful lot like every other relationship in the world? We should care about our answer to that question far more than any friend, parent, or pastor.

Rest in Grace, Fight by Faith

Two banners hang over all our dating and over every accountability relationship. First, Paul promises us, "There is therefore now no condemnation for those who are in Christ Jesus" (Rom. 8:1). Good accountability, grounded in the gospel, does not breed condemnation but confidence. It reminds us that we are saved by grace alone through faith alone in Christ alone. Nothing we do earns God's love and protection. And if we are in Christ, nothing can separate us from his love. The gospel is big enough to cover all our sin, no matter how far we have run from God, and to redeem us from any of our mistakes or failures in dating.

Second, Paul promises, "If you live according to the flesh you will die, but if by the Spirit you put to death the deeds of the body, you will live" (Rom. 8:13). Life and death are at stake in everything we do. Are we living to please ourselves and our sinful desires, or are we killing sin wherever we find it? We draw others into our dating—the third wheel we all need—because we want our lives, relationships, and marriages to count for Christ, and because we can't risk the devastating consequences of letting sin persist or thrive anywhere in our hearts.

16

It's Not You—It's God

When did you get your own cell phone? My friends started getting them in junior high. Therefore, of course, I wanted one, too. No, I *needed* my own phone. That was the case I made to Mom and Dad on a nightly basis, anyway. I mean, how was I supposed to live in this world, at thirteen, without a phone? I had all kinds of important calls to make. "And what if I was in trouble and needed to reach you guys . . . ?" That was always the desperate Hail Mary when the conversation seemed to be going south. My parents held the line—literally. They promised they would buy me a phone when I turned sixteen and could drive. Before then, no phone.

After three long years crawling in the desert of disconnection, shackled to our home phone like a corded teenager, I spotted the cool spring of my sixteenth birthday. Christmas came, just one month before my birthday. I looked through the pile of presents under the tree, and I knew my flip-phone freedom was hiding in there somewhere. My brothers and I started unwrapping gifts. My mom and dad immediately handed me a box. I knew this was it. I was finally becoming a man. I ripped off the paper, and behold, my very first cell phone.

I looked at it for a few seconds, the thing I had waited and begged for *for years*. It wasn't what I expected. It was bigger than my friends' phones. We're talking pre-smartphone big here—not cool. And it didn't have any games on it—not one. It was kind of, well, plain and boring.

Everyone kept opening presents, and I started to feel slighted. It seemed that my brothers were getting more presents, and better presents. I felt that my parents were punishing me. "Marshall, can you hand this to Cam?" "Marshall, pass that over to Noah." Golf clubs, a stereo, and gift cards to Chipotle. I was getting socks, underwear, and the classic Mom sweater. I almost started to cry. Sixteen years old and about to throw a pity party, a tantrum. The state of Ohio was prepared to let me operate a car driving 65-plus miles per hour, and there I was, crying on Christmas morning.

My brothers opened their last gifts. We cleaned up the wrapping paper while Mom got breakfast ready. Disappointed, I collected my new undies. We sat down at the table to eat. Dad said he forgot something in the trunk of his car and asked me to grab it. *Are you serious? After what you did to me in there?* "Sure, I'll grab it." I walked into the garage, opened the trunk, and there was nothing there. *You've got to be kidding me.* Just as I was about to slam the trunk shut, the garage door opened behind me. I turned around and saw a bright, silver Volkswagen Jetta with a big red bow sitting on top. I almost fainted. My parents had bought a third car so that I would have one to drive when I got my license. I forgot I even had a phone. I immediately jumped in with my dad. I was wearing cow slippers. Yes, sixteen, and wearing cow slippers. We drove around for twenty minutes. We were the only people on the highway that morning. I smiled every inch, every turn, even every red light. I had spent the last three years fixated on a phone, craving a phone, all while my parents secretly wanted to buy a car for me.

God's Love in Unrequited Love

The emotional roller coaster of that Christmas morning is a light-hearted and fun picture of a hard reality. God often withholds, or even takes away, something from us in order to give us something far greater. Our Father in heaven knows all our needs, has plans for us we never could have imagined for ourselves, and wields the whole universe for our good. But doing what's best for us often requires causing us some pain or discomfort first, like drilling a cavity or resetting a bone. God's love can be unpleasant, even excruciating in the moment, but it always steers us through every dark valley to unparalleled life and joy. It also saves us all kinds of grief and pain in the future.

Pain is never evidence that God forgot about us or doesn't care anymore. He promises, "Fear not, for I am with you; be not dismayed, for I am your God; I will strengthen you, I will help you, I will uphold you with my righteous right hand" (Isa. 41:10). If he allows us to walk through something hard or painful, like a breakup, he walks with us every step and waits on the other side to give us a gift that dwarfs all our suffering—like trading an uncool cell phone for a new car. Paul says, "This light momentary affliction is preparing for us an eternal weight of glory beyond all comparison" (2 Cor. 4:17).

Breakups are often our first taste of love like that, and most of us wouldn't order seconds. Some of a single person's darkest days fall after a breakup. You risked your heart. You shared your life. You bought the gifts, made the memories, and dreamed your dreams *together*—and it fell apart. Now, you're back at square one in the quest for marriage, and it feels lonelier than square one, and further from the altar because of all you've spent and lost. *What if every relationship ends like this? What if I never marry?* To the brokenhearted and afraid, God says, "Fear not, for I have redeemed you; I have called you by name, you are mine. When you pass through the waters, I will be with you; and through the rivers, they shall not overwhelm you; when you walk through fire you shall not be burned, and the flame shall not consume you" (Is. 43:1–2). Breakups are often the deepest waters and the warmest fires in the not-yet-married life. But if we will trust God and run to him in our heartache and confusion, it's in those waters and fires that we will experience his nearness and love like never before.

Seven Lessons for Any Breakup

The reality is that good, Christ-exalting relationships very often fail before the ceremony, never to be recovered romantically. The pain cuts deep and lingers long. Breakups in the church are painful and uncomfortable, and many of us have walked or will walk this dark and lonely road at some point. So here are seven lessons for building hope and loving others when Christians end a not-yet-married relationship.

1. It's okay to cry—and you probably should.

Breakups almost always hurt. Maybe you didn't see it coming, and the other person suddenly wants out. Maybe you were convinced it needed to end but knew how hard it would be to tell her. Maybe you've been together for years. Maybe you love his family and friends. Without the ceremony and marriage vows, it's *not* a divorce, but it can feel like it.

It feels like divorce for a reason. You weren't made for this kind of misery. God engineered romance to be expressed in fidelity and loyalty—in oneness. Because dating is only a means to *marriage*, God's design for marriage tells us about his design for dating. Dating that dives in too quickly or dumps too carelessly does not reflect God's intention. This doesn't mean every dating relationship should end in marriage, but it does mean breakups will hurt. God created you to enjoy and thrive in love that lasts, like Christ's lasting love for his bride. So feel free to feel, and know that the pain points to something beautiful about your God and his undying love for you.

And if it doesn't hurt, it probably should. If we can come in and out of relationships without pain or remorse, something is likely out of sync. This doesn't mean we have to be ruined by every breakup, but there should be a sense that it's not how it's supposed to be. Hearts weren't built to be borrowed. God needs to show some of us the gravity of failed relationships because of what they wrongly suggest about him and his love for the church.

2. Don't try again too quickly.

Knowing and embracing God's design for permanence in marriage and dating will help us to handle our feelings appropriately, but it will also help us take healthy next steps in our pursuit of marriage. One of the worst and most popular mistakes is moving on to the next one too soon. Especially in the age of online dating and social media, we really don't have to work very hard to find another prospect.

Affection can be an addiction. If you've been on dates, held hands, seen smiles, exchanged texts, and experienced the sweetness of another's attention and affirmation, you will want more. And the easiest way to find it is to rebound right away. But if we care about God, our witness, our ex, and our future significant other, we'll wait, pray, and date patiently and carefully. It's too easy to leave behind a trail of wounded people in our pursuit of a partner. It's a lie to think that we're not moving toward marriage if we're not dating someone right now. Sometimes the best thing we can do for our future spouse is not date. If your history looks serial, you might need to break up with dating for a while. It can be a time to regroup, grow, and discover a new rhythm for your future relationship.

3. You are better having loved and lost.

There's a unique shame and brokenness associated with breakups. Relationships and love may be celebrated more in the church than anywhere else because we (rightly) love marriage so much. Unfortunately, these same convictions often make breakups an uncomfortable conversation—at best embarrassing and at worst scandalous or humiliating. You feel like damaged goods, like you've been ruined in God's eyes or in the eyes of others. The hard-to-believe but beautiful truth is that broken-up you *is* a better you. When in your sorrow you turn to the Lord and repent of whatever sin you brought to the relationship, you will find that you are as precious to your heavenly Father as you have ever been, and he is using every inch of your heartache, failure, and regret to make you more of what he created you to be, and to give you more of what he created you to enjoy—himself.

When one prize is stripped away, we can graciously be reminded of how little we have apart from Christ *and* the fortune he's purchased for us with his blood. He has become for us wisdom for the foolish, righteousness for sinners, sanctification for the broken, and redemption for the lost and afraid (1 Cor. 1:30)—and affection and security and identity for the lonely man or woman reeling after the end of a relationship. In Jesus, God is always and only doing good to us. He loves our lasting joy in him much more than he loves our temporary comfort today. He'll make the trade any day, and we can be glad he does. Know that God *is* doing good, even when we feel the worst.

4. Learn from any love lost.

One of Satan's greatest victories in a breakup is convincing a guy or girl, "It was all the other person's fault." The reality is no one—married or not—is without sin or fault in a relationship. Saved by grace, we are all flawed and filled with the Spirit, so we will all always be learning and growing as people and spouses—present or future. After the emotional tidal wave has crashed and passed, take some time alone and then with close friends to assess where God is carrying you—who he's making you to be—through this.

Identify an area or areas where you want to strive to be more gracious, more discerning, or more faithful—more like Jesus—moving forward. You won't experience many relational crossroads more intense, personal, and specific than a breakup, so it truly is a unique time for some hopeful, healthy introspection, checked and balanced by some other believers.

5. Even if you can't be friends now, you will be siblings forever.
For Christian relationships, breakups are never the end. Whether it sounds appealing now or not, you *will* be together forever (Rev. 7:9–10). And you'll do so in a new world where no one is married, and everyone is happy. Jesus says, "In the resurrection they neither marry nor are given in marriage" (Matt. 22:30). Psalm 16:11 says, "In your presence there is fullness of joy; at your right hand are pleasures forevermore." Sounds too good to be true, right? So what would it mean to move on and think about our ex in light of eternity? While you will meet again and forever in heaven, you may not be able to be friends now. And that is not necessarily sinful. In fact, in many cases, it might be healthy emotionally and spiritually to create some significant space and boundaries. Hearts that have been given away, at whatever level, need to heal and develop new expectations.

Reconciliation does not require closeness. It *does* require forgiveness and brotherly love. You could start by praying for your exes, even when you can't handle talking to them. Pray that their faith would increase, that God would bring believing brothers or sisters around them, that he would heal and restore their hearts, that he would make them more like Jesus. We need to learn to live today in our relationships, old and new, in light of our eternity together. Our patience, kindness, and forgiveness in breakups will shine beautifully next to the selfish, vindictive responses modeled in reality TV and adopted thoughtlessly by the rest of the world.

6. *"It's not you, it's God" is not enough.*

It might be one of the most popular Christian breakup lines: "God is leading me to do this." "God told me we need to break up." "I saw a vision in a bush on my way to class, and we weren't together." All of them can probably be summed up like this: "Look, it's not you, it's God." God very well may lead you to a breakup, but don't use him as a scapegoat. Own your own sin and ask for forgiveness where it is needed. Then be honest about how you came to this decision, how God made this direction clear to you. Sure, some things will be intangible, but find the tangible factors. This is not a license to say harmful things, but helpful things, even if they may hurt initially.

It's wise not to be alone in your opinion about the need to break up. Yes, your boyfriend or girlfriend might not agree, but you need to share and confirm your perspective with someone who loves Jesus and both of you. Go to someone you know who can assess your heart in wanting to get out. If it can be a married man or woman, all the better. Talk to someone who knows what it takes to persevere in marriage and see what they think about your "deal breaker(s)" in the relationship.

Our imagination, especially in an emotional crisis, can be a lethal weapon that Satan leverages against us for evil. When we leave everything vague and spiritual, our ex will not, and the majority of what his mind creates will be lies from the Devil. Give him enough information about how God led you to this decision without crushing him or tearing him down. I say "enough" because there are lots of true but unhelpful things you could say. Again, run your talking points past a Christian brother or sister before taking them to your soon-to-be ex. In the end, he doesn't have to agree with you, but it's loving to help him toward the clarity and closure you're feeling. It just may free him to grow and move forward sooner and with fewer questions.

7. *Your Father knows your needs.*

You're probably questioning this in the wake of your breakup, but God does know what you need, and he's never too slow to provide it. He might reveal new things to you about what you thought you needed. Or he might simply show you how much more you need him than anything or anyone else. God feeds the unemployed birds of the air (Matt. 6:26). God grows the flowers of the field and makes them beautiful, even though they'll be cut, stomped, eaten, or frozen in a matter of days or weeks (Matt. 6:28–30). How much more will this Father care and provide for his blood-bought children?

One way God provides for us through breakups is by making clear—by whatever means and for whatever reason—that this relationship was not his plan for our marriage. The heart of Christian dating is looking for clarity more than intimacy. This probably won't taste sweet in the moment, but if you treasure clarity, breakups won't be all bad news. We all know some of the news we need most is hardest for a time but better down the road. A breakup may feel like unwrapping a few fresh pairs of underwear for Christmas, but we have to admit that God will always give us better gifts than we would give ourselves. He knows more than we do, and he loves us even more than we love ourselves.

Joy in the Shadows of Heartbreak

When we're left alone and feeling abandoned, it's really hard to believe anyone knows what we're going through. That may even be true of the good-intentioned people around you. It is not true of Jesus. This Jesus came and was broken to give hope to the broken. "A bruised reed he will not break, and a smoldering wick he will not quench, until he brings justice to victory" (Matt. 12:20). The joy is not in knowing that Jesus had it hard too—not much comfort there. The joy is in knowing that the one who suffered in your place died and rose again to end suffering for his saints. For those who hope in Jesus, all pain—unexpected cancer, unfair criticism, an unwanted breakup—was given an expiration date and repurposed until then to unite us in love to our suffering Savior.

Jesus went before the brokenhearted to pave the way for joy in pain. We live, survive, and thrive by looking to him, "who for the joy that was set before him endured the cross" (Heb. 12:2). His joy before the wrath of God against sin is our first and greatest reason to fight for joy—not just survival—after a breakup. If you believe that, then make the most of any breakup, knowing God has chosen this particular path to grow and gratify you in ways that last. No relationship you have in this life will last forever, but the good things that happen through them in you—even through their sorrows, yes even through their collapses—will.

Conclusion

My Dreams for Your Marriage

Her big day had finally come, the day she had been planning since she was five—a ceremony twenty-five years in the making. As the last guests arrived and the bridal party lined up, she sat out of sight by herself in a side room, waiting for the big reveal.

She stared at the old wooden door separating her from all her friends and family. The minutes crawled along like hours. A tear fell out of the corner of her eye, and walked down her cheek. It caught her off guard, like an unexpected and uninvited guest. Was it because the day was here at last, her long-awaited groom waiting for her by the altar—the ecstasy of finally wearing white after all those bridesmaid dresses? Or, as she began to be honest with herself, was she crying because her wedding was nothing like what she thought it would be? Was it that *she* was not the bride she thought she'd be?

She had thought she'd be married by now. When she was younger, she tried to be patient and do things the right way. But no guy ever showed interest—most of them not even enough to know her name. They always went after the prettier girls and the ones ready to fool around sexually. She could still remember the pain of lying in bed at night, scrolling through social media, wondering if her relationship status would ever change.

Tired of waiting around and missing out, she broke up with her old standards. She started dating more aggressively her first year in college and never really stopped. She couldn't remember a time when she didn't have a boyfriend. She could remember every breakup—every ounce of heartbreak. The wounds still hurt, even on her wedding day—even with a fiancé waiting fifty yards away. Her fiancé. What if he knew everything about her past? What if he could have heard her say, "I love you," to all those other men? What if he knew how far things had gone, how she had let each new guy push the boundaries? Would he still say, "I do"? She was happy she had found her man—she really was—but devastated she hadn't saved herself. She had gone about it all wrong and couldn't leave her history behind. She took another nervous look in the mirror and suddenly felt more uncomfortable in white.

She secretly dreaded those first weeks and months of marriage. Sure, the honeymoon would be fun, but what about real life? *What will he think about me when he really gets to know me, when he sees all my flaws and weaknesses up close?* She was terrified they might end up like her parents and that her children might suffer like she had—stuck between two homes, torn between Mom and Dad. She had always thought marriage might complete her, that it might fill out her purpose in life and give her the happiness she had chased for so long. Moments before saying her vows, she knew she was wrong. And now she was about to parade down the aisle with false hopes and unfulfilled expectations, the room filled with beautiful white roses to help her forget her failures and lots of do-it-yourself decorations to distract her from all her shame and fear.

She heard her song, the one she had been hearing in her imagination since she was a little girl. A knock at the door signaled it was time. She stood, straightened her dress, wiped the tear or two from her face, and smiled. She had picked the dress and her makeup, but she never knew she would have to put on a smile. She was happy, but she couldn't stop thinking about all she had done wrong. As she opened the door and stepped into the aisle, she was totally unprepared for what was waiting there for her.

What Dreams Do You Have for Marriage?

Have you thought much about your wedding day and the marriage on the other side? The day Faye and I got married, we already knew people were going to ask us how marriage was going—in a month, or a year, or ten years—and we didn't want to have to settle for how we felt in the moment. So we prayed about what we wanted out of marriage. We had specific, hope-filled dreams for what God might do as we patiently and selflessly gave ourselves to one another day after day until death do us part. We walked the aisle looking beyond the altar, our beautiful bridal party, and all our beloved guests to something far bigger and more significant: a lifetime of treasuring Christ together in marriage. For sure, even one year in, we're still naïve and inexperienced, but we have a God bigger than all our fears, inadequacies, and future failures. The marriage in our imaginations is not always pretty, but it is beautiful. It's not always easy, but it is worth all the effort and sacrifice. It's certainly not perfect, but it is filled with grace and joy.

We have seventeen dreams for our marriage, and they're the same dreams I have for yours. I wonder if you have dreams for your marriage? A marriage without a vision might survive, but it probably won't grow or thrive. And if we date without some specific desires and goals for our marriage, we'll probably settle for something less and wake up one day wondering why our marriage isn't what we thought it would be. Whether you're currently married, in a serious relationship, or simply feel called to be married someday, God created marriage to be an amazingly rich, dynamic, and fruitful experience for his children. Pray and ask him to show you new and deeper dimensions of all he means marriage to be for you and your (future) spouse.

1. May we enjoy God more than anyone or anything else, including each other (Ps. 16:11).
2. May we pray and pray and pray (Matt. 6:9–13).
3. May we have and raise joyful, godly children, if God wills (Ps. 127:3–4).
4. May we be bold ambassadors for the gospel wherever we go and always be winning worshipers for him (2 Cor. 5:20).
5. May we meet God together regularly in his Word (Ps. 19:7–10).
6. May we make our home a safe, inviting, and life-giving place for others (Rom. 12:13).
7. May we be a blessing to the families God has given to us (Eph. 6:1–3).
8. May we find ways to learn from marriages more mature than ours and to invest in marriages younger than ours (Eph. 5:18–25).
9. May we live worthy of the gospel, cultivating shorter cycles of correction, confession, repentance, forgiveness, and reconciliation (Heb. 3:12–13).
10. May we develop, enjoy, guard, and model a healthy and pure sex life (Phil. 2:3–5).
11. May we maintain a healthy rhythm of rest, knowing that God loves us and runs the world (Ps. 127:1–2).
12. May we always love and invest in the local church (Heb. 10:24–25).
13. May we disciple younger men and women and raise up leaders for God's church (2 Tim. 2:1–2).
14. May we support God's global cause through world missions (Ps. 67:3–4).
15. May we hold what we have loosely and overflow freely in generosity (2 Cor. 9:7–8).
16. May we sing (Ps. 5:11).

17. May we never stop pursuing each other, striving to know and serve each other faithfully and creatively (Rom. 12:10).

The list is long but not complete. It's our weak and creative attempt to maximize our greater purpose in life—to reveal some of God's beauty, sufficiency, and worth—and to chase as much happiness in him together as possible. We have no doubt that there are more and better dreams to dream. But for now, after a year of running after these seventeen things, we know how to pray tomorrow. Our greatest desire is for God himself, so we have every confidence that he will lead us, meet us, and keep us in marriage.

Dreams Change How We Date

Most of us don't stop to really think about marriage while we're dating. A lot of us have probably thought a lot *about* marriage, but have we really thought *through* marriage? We may have thought through geography (*Where will we live?*), finances (*Will we be poor?*), sex (*Will I still be attracted to him or her?*), and maybe even children (*How many kids do we want?*). But day-in, day-out life together in marriage is not consumed by any of those desires or questions. They all get answered pretty quickly and only come up occasionally afterward—even as serious and important as those questions are.

What does that mean for dating? While we're getting to know someone and pursuing clarity about whether we might marry, we should be thinking about following Jesus in everyday life together in marriage. I'm not talking mainly about date nights, or your sex life, or your shared hobbies or interests. I'm talking about chasing after Jesus and spending your lives for his sake, laying down your life, your marriage, and your family day after day to serve others and lead them to him. Set your sights higher. Expect more of each other. Pursue and build a marriage that makes more of Jesus than you could have by yourself. Date and marry with specific dreams in mind.

Her Dream Wedding

As she stepped into the aisle, filled with fear and shame, she saw her groom. Suddenly, it was if no one else was in the room, just the two of them staring into each other's eyes. He didn't say a word, but his face said everything she needed to hear. His eyes told her he knew it all, every inch of her past—every lonely night, every bad decision, every unhealthy relationship, every sexual act—and that he had still chosen her and loved her as his wife. She may not have deserved to wear white that day, but he had bought the dress for her, to cover all her failures. His smile told her she was forgiven and prized—the delight of his eyes. She forgot ever feeling unnoticed or unwanted. A tear fell out of the corner of his eye and walked down his cheek. It melted away all her shame and fear. She had found her groom, the one willing to die for her, on a cross, "that he might present [her] to himself in splendor, without spot or wrinkle or any such thing, that she might be holy and without blemish" (Eph. 5:27).

We are the sinful and broken bride, filled with regret, fear, and shame—regardless of whether we have a dating history or a sexual past—and Jesus stands at the end of the aisle waiting to undo all we've done wrong and to welcome us into a love and relationship beyond our most romantic imaginations. On this side of heaven, we are all not yet married. We are all waiting for a day, after the last wedding has finished—after the last walk down the aisle, the last wedding cake, the last first dance—when as one family we will meet our groom. At *that* wedding we will sing, "Let us rejoice and exult and give him the glory, for the marriage of the Lamb has come, and his Bride has made herself ready" (Rev. 19:7). For many of us, marriage will have its day, but it will feel like only a day, next to an eternity with our Savior and King. We will stare at Jesus—without shame, without guilt, without sadness, without fear—and experience the first moments of a happiness unlike any here on earth. We *will* all be married, and that marriage has everything to do with how we live, date, and marry now.

Notes

1. John Piper first introduced me to this idea in his sermon "Why Did God Create the World?," September 22, 2012, Desiring God website, http://www.desiringgod.org/messages/why-did-god-create-the-world.
2. John Piper, *Desiring God: Meditations of a Christian Hedonist*, rev. ed. (Colorado Springs: Multnomah, 2011), 288.
3. John Piper, *God Is the Gospel: Meditations on God's Love as the Gift of Himself* (Wheaton, IL: Crossway, 2005), 47.
4. David Platt, *Radical: Taking Back Your Faith from the American Dream* (Colorado Springs: Multnomah, 2010), 105.
5. For more on the battle against sexual lust and pornography, you can read my article "Never Harmless, Never Private, Never Safe," Desiring God website, http://www.desiringgod.org/articles/never-harmless-never-private-never-safe.
6. When should young people begin to date? I address that question in my article "Wait to Date Until You Can Marry," Desiring God website, http://www.desiringgod.org/articles/wait-to-date-until-you-can-marry.
7. Timothy Keller, *The Meaning of Marriage: Facing the Complexities of Commitment with the Wisdom of God* (New York: Dutton, 2011), 109, 120–21, 123.
8. Ibid., 87.
9. For more on the role of physical attraction, you can read my article "Isn't She Beautiful?," Desiring God website, http://www.desiringgod.org/articles/isn-t-she-beautiful.
10. Keller, *Meaning of Marriage*, 222.
11. For more about the role of dads in dating, you can read my article "Dads, Date Your Daughter's Boyfriend," Desiring God website, http://www.desiringgod.org/articles/dads-date-your-daughter-s-boyfriend.

A Word of Thanks

I don't know which part of *Not Yet Married* will be the most memorable for readers. I do know that this page of thanks was my favorite to write.

Desiring God has been my writing home, but that barely begins to describe its influence in my life. In a 2006 message, John Piper painted the biggest picture of God I had ever seen, and he hasn't stopped driving my joy in God higher and deeper. David Mathis has been a wise and faithful mentor and advocate, and a far better friend. Stefan Green, Tony Reinke, Jonathan Parnell, Jon Bloom, and Phillip Holmes walked with me one article at a time, sharpened my thinking, and made me laugh a lot along the way.

Crossway graciously opened a door for me to publish my first book. They have been great partners at every step. Special thanks to Lydia Brownback for the line-by-line love she poured into every chapter. Only I know just how well she served you.

God used several key men to strengthen and refine me through my not-yet-married life. Some were married, others were single, but all were pivotal in pointing me to Jesus. Bryan, Kevin, Dieudonné, Eric, Dan, and Ben shaped me as a man more than most.

But the two strongest, most devoted pillars in my not-yet-married story were my parents. There is simply no unit of measurement to begin to quantify the role Mom and Dad had in this book. Their personality, their conviction, their humor, their love, their wisdom, and their patience color the ink on page after page.

Alyssa Faye, my *Not Yet Married* journey ended and began with you. You were the stunning, forgiving, and loving last stop on my long road to marriage. But from before I typed my first word, you also were, and continue to be, the greatest champion of this book. This book is *our* story. These chapters are filled with lessons we learned together. Every page represents *our* dream for the not yet married. Thank you for all you joyfully sacrificed to build this book with me.

If there is anything of true and real and lasting value in the book, it has come only from God. Any meaningful change in your singleness and dating will also be from him and through him and to him (Rom. 11:36). All the treasures of wisdom and knowledge—every inch and every ounce for every part of life—are hidden in him (Col. 2:3). I wrote because of what he has done in my life, praying that he will do the same and more in yours. He truly deserves all the thanks.

General Index

advice, 176
affection, 185
anxiety, 45, 49, 50, 51, 53, 87; in
     marriage, 46
appetites, 25
aspirations, 78–83
attraction, physical, 143–45

Bible, the, 61; best book on dating,
     116–25; about God, 119–20;
     marriage in, 106
boundaries, 112–13, 154; conversa-
     tional, 164–65; in dating, 160,
     168–69; emotional, 163; physi-
     cal, 162–63, 165–67; redefin-
     ing, 161–62
boyfriends, responsibilities of,
     167–69
breakups, 54–55, 183; lessons for,
     184–89; shame in, 185–86
burdens, 172–73

calling, 71–72, 77, 83; confirmation
     of, 134; to marriage, 134–35,
     143; sense of, 142; to single-
     ness, 133–35
cares, 44, 50–51
children, raising, 131–32
Christian life: as fight, 25; mission
     of, 18, 35; responsibilities of, 35
Christians: as bride of Christ, 196;
     and connection, 68; as family,
     74; God's plans for, 40

church, the, 71, 82; as family,
     174–76; healthy, 72; as place
     of salvation, 82; serving, 82–83
clarity, 145; in dating, 189, 195;
     pursuit of, 137, 140, 141–42,
     146
commitment, 89
community: and dating, 113–14;
     importance of, 68, 71, 74
compatibility, 108–9, 135
contentment, in Jesus, 65
conversion, 34
cross, the, 151; cheapening, 154

dating, 11–12, 105–15; account-
     ability in, 173; Christian,
     162; clarity in, 189, 195; in
     community, 113–14; confu-
     sion in, 140; desire for, 129;
     goal of, 124; God's design
     for, 184–85; independence
     in, 162; intimacy in, 140–41;
     leadership in, 168–69; toward
     marriage, 110–11, 112; and
     ministry, 179; missionary, 114;
     prize in, 110; purpose for, 110;
     questions in, 146–47; risks in,
     109–10
desire: for dating, 129; for God,
     142–43, 195
Devil, the. See Satan
disappointment, 62–63, 65, 69

200

discernment, in dating, 109, 140–43
distractions, 42–43, 44–45, 46, 47,
    49; as blinding, 44; in mar-
    riage, 46–47; three labels for,
    44
divorce, 14, 108, 127, 129, 140,
    184

entitlement, 88
expectations, 62

failure: confessing, 174, 178; in
    marriage, 139; redemption
    from, 180, 186, 192, 196;
    sexual, 128, 156–58
faith: threat to, 44; in trials, 59
faithfulness, to Jesus, 172–73
friendship, 71, 72–73, 163, 171,
    177–78; need for, 174

generosity, 82
gentleness, 90
glorifying God, 29–30, 42, 48,
    78–79; by work, 81
God: care of, 57–58, 189; as
    creator, 27, 61; as Father,
    53; gifts of, 183; as giver, 45;
    goodness of, 65, 186; grace
    of, 180; knowing, 155; love
    of, 26, 31–32, 160, 177, 184,
    189; omniscient, 53, 189;
    plans of, 65, 96–97; power of,
    160; provider, 81; purposes
    of, 18, 32, 34; resisting, 61;
    satisfied in, 80; as source
    of marriage, 121–22, 124;
    sovereignty of, 40; as subject
    of Scripture, 119–20; trust in,
    154–55; will of, 29, 31; and
    work, 78–79
godliness, growth in, 85–86
Google, 170–71
gospel, the: abuses of, 36; and mar-
    riage, 133, 142; and work, 78
Great Commission, the, 34–35

happiness, 23, 29, 32
heaven, 48–49
hell, 48–49
hoarding, 82
holiness, 88–89
Holy Spirit, the: filled with, 186;
    fruit of, 86, 88, 91–93; help
    of, 120; life in, 89; pray-
    ing through, 95; walking by,
    172–73; work of, 38, 132
hope, 62
"Hope for the Unhappy Single"
    (Segal), 70
humility, 61
husbands, as leaders, 167–68

identity, 53
idolatry, 90
idol(s), 62–63; as marriage, 123;
    as plans, 62; as relationships,
    24
impatience, 87–88
independence, 66–67; in dating,
    162
infatuation, 123
intimacy, 137, 146; appetite for,
    113; danger in, 138–39, 140;
    in dating, 140–41; desire for,
    138; as gift, 138; before mar-
    riage, 110, 113; in marriage,
    161; as prize, 139; purpose for,
    124
investments, 83
Isaac and Rebekah, 120–24
isolation, 67–68, 69, 72, 90

Jesus Christ, 15, 35; authority of,
    36; as Bridegroom, 14–15,
    92; death of, 135–36; glory
    of, 34; hope in, 190; know-
    ing, 59; love of, 180; patience
    of, 60; pursuit of, 195; return
    of, 48–49; as satisfying, 49;
    serving, 79; suffering of, 62;

Scripture Index